HARCOURT SCIENCE

WORKBOOK

Harcourt School Publishers

Orlando • Boston • Dallas • Chicago • San Diego

www.harcourtschool.com

Contents

Safety in Science

Doing investigations in science can be fun, but you need to be sure you do them safely. Here are some rules to follow.

1 **Think ahead.** Study the steps of the investigation so you know what to expect. If you have any questions, ask your teacher. Be sure you understand any safety symbols that are shown.

2 **Be neat.** Keep your work area clean. If you have long hair, pull it back so it doesn't get in the way. Roll or push up long sleeves to keep them away from your experiment.

3 **Oops!** If you should spill or break something or get cut, tell your teacher right away.

4 **Watch your eyes.** Wear safety goggles anytime you are directed to do so. If you get anything in your eyes, tell your teacher right away.

5 **Yuck!** Never eat or drink anything during a science activity unless you are told to do so by your teacher.

6 **Don't get shocked.** Be especially careful if an electric appliance is used. Be sure that electric cords are in a safe place where you can't trip over them. Don't ever pull a plug out of an outlet by pulling on the cord.

7 **Keep it clean.** Always clean up when you have finished. Put everything away and wipe your work area. Wash your hands.

In some activities you will see these symbols. They are signs for what you need to act safely.

CAUTION
Be especially careful.

CAUTION
Wear safety goggles.

CAUTION
Be careful with sharp objects.

CAUTION
Don't get burned.

CAUTION
Protect your clothes.

CAUTION
Protect your hands with mitts.

CAUTION
Be careful with electricity.

Science Safety

_____ I will study the steps of the investigation before I begin.

_____ I will ask my teacher if I do not understand something.

_____ I will keep my work area clean.

_____ I will pull my hair back and roll up long sleeves before I begin.

_____ I will tell my teacher if I spill or break something or get cut.

_____ I will wear safety goggles when I am told to do so.

_____ I will tell my teacher if I get something in my eye.

_____ I will not eat or drink anything during an investigation unless told to do so by my teacher.

_____ I will be extra careful when using electrical appliances.

_____ I will keep electric cords out of the way and only unplug them by pulling on the protected plug.

_____ I will clean up when I am finished.

_____ I will return unused materials to my teacher.

_____ I will wipe my area and then wash my hands.

Chapter 1 • Graphic Organizer for Chapter Concepts

Living Things

LESSON 1 CELLS	LESSON 2 FEATURES OF ANIMALS	LESSON 3 FEATURES OF PLANTS WITH SEEDS	LESSON 4 FEATURES OF FUNGI
Cells are _____	Animals are classified according to body plan as:	Two kinds of plants make seeds. They are:	The cells of fungi have
Animal cells have these parts:	1. _____ or _____	1. _____	1. _____ like plants,
1. _____	2. _____	and _____	2. but they do not have
2. _____	Animals are classified according to body structures as:	2. _____	The cells fungi use for reproduction are called
3. _____	1. _____ or _____		1. _____
4. _____	2. _____		Examples of fungi include:
Plant cells have the same parts, plus:			1. _____
1. _____ or _____			2. _____
2. _____			3. _____
Living things may have:			4. _____
1. _____ or _____			
2. _____			

Name _____

Date _____

Make a Model Cell

Materials

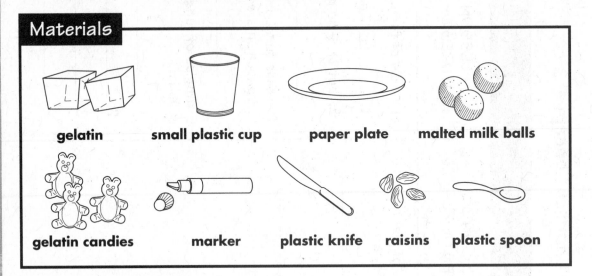

gelatin   small plastic cup   paper plate   malted milk balls

gelatin candies   marker   plastic knife   raisins   plastic spoon

Activity Procedure

1 Use the marker to write your group's name on a plastic cup. Then, pour the liquid gelatin your teacher provides into the plastic cup until it is two-thirds full. Allow the gelatin to chill until set.

2 Gently remove the gelatin from the cup. Use the knife to slice the gelatin mold in half. Place the gelatin halves on a paper plate. The gelatin is the cytoplasm of your cell. *Cytoplasm* is a jellylike material that fills the space of a cell.

3 Using the spoon, make a small hole in the center of one of the gelatin halves. Place the malted milk ball in the hole. This is your cell's nucleus. The *nucleus* determines the cell's activities. See Picture A on page A5.

4 Scatter a few raisins and gelatin candies within the cytoplasm. The raisins represent the structures that release energy for the cell (mitochondria). The candies are storage areas for the cell (vacuoles). See Picture B on page A5.

5 Carefully place the plain half of the gelatin on top of the half that contains the cell parts. Your cell is now ready to observe.

Name _____

Draw Conclusions

1. **Observe** your model. What cell part makes up the greatest part of your model? What can you conclude from this observation?

   _____

2. What cell part is in the center of your cell?

   _____

   Where in the cell are all the other cell parts located?

   _____

   _____

3. **Scientists at Work** Scientists often use **models** to better understand complex structures. How does your cell model help you **draw conclusions** about the structure of cells? What things about a cell does your model NOT tell you?

   _____

   _____

   _____

   _____

Investigate Further Make a drawing of your cell model, and label each part with the name of the cell part it represents. Then compare your model to the pictures of the cells on pages A7 and A8. How are the drawings similar? How are they different?

   _____

   _____

   _____

   _____

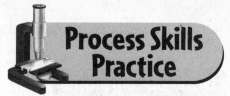

Using a Model to Draw Conclusions

Plant cells have an extra part. The chloroplasts give plants their green color. Repeat your experiment, adding some green olives to the mixture. Draw the plant cells below. What further conclusions can you draw, based on this new model? Label the cell parts in your drawing.

Summarize and Paraphrase

Fill in the outline below with the major points of the text on pages A8–A9. When you have finished, write a summary of each section, combining the major points.

I. Plant Cells

    A. Differences of cells:

    _____

    _____

    B. Parts of cells:

    _____

    _____

    C. Chloroplasts:

    _____

    _____

II. One-Celled Microorganisms

    A. Definition:

    _____

    _____

    B. Function of cell parts:

    _____

    _____

Summary of Plant Cells:

_____

_____

_____

Summary of One-Celled Microorganisms:

_____

_____

_____

Name _____

Date _____

 **Concept Review**

What Are Cells?

Lesson Concept

One or more cells make up all living things. The smallest one-celled living things are microorganisms. Every cell has smaller parts to keep the cell alive.

Use the following vocabulary terms to complete each sentence below.

Vocabulary

cell (A6)   **cell membrane** (A7)   **cytoplasm** (A7)

nucleus (A7)   **cell wall** (A8)   **chloroplasts** (A8)

microorganisms (A9)

1. A jellylike substance filling most of the space in a cell is called

_____ .

2. The _____ keeps the cell firm and gives a

plant support.

3. The basic unit of all living things is a _____ .

4. Because they are tiny one-celled plants and animals,

_____ can be seen only with a microscope.

5. A _____ encloses a cell and gives it shape.

6. _____ help plants make food.

7. The "brain" of the cell is the _____ .

Explain the differences between plant and animal cells.

_____

_____

_____

_____

Name _____

Date _____

Comparing Real and Artificial Sponges

Materials

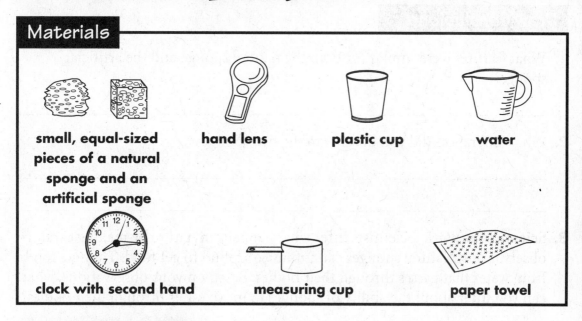

small, equal-sized pieces of a natural sponge and an artificial sponge

hand lens

plastic cup

water

clock with second hand

measuring cup

paper towel

Activity Procedure

1 Make a chart like the one below.

Characteristic	Natural Sponge	Artificial Sponge
What it looks like		
What it feels like		
How heavy it feels		
How much water it holds		

2 **Observe** each piece of sponge to see how it looks and feels. **Record** your observations in the chart.

3 Use a hand lens to **observe** each piece of sponge more closely. **Record** your observations in the chart. You may wish to use drawings to record some of your observations. See Picture A on page A13.

4 Half-fill the plastic cup with water. Put the natural sponge in the cup and push it down into the water. Allow the sponge to remain in the water for 30 seconds.

5 Remove the sponge from the cup. Hold the sponge over the measuring cup and squeeze out the water in the sponge. **Record** in your chart the amount of water held by the sponge. See Picture B on page A13.

6 Repeat steps 4 and 5 for the artificial sponge.

Draw Conclusions

1. What features were similar for both the natural sponge and the artificial sponge?

_____

2. What differences did you observe in the two sponges?

_____

_____

3. Scientists at Work Scientists **infer** what happens in nature by making careful observations. Natural sponges cannot move around to get food. They get food from water that passes through their bodies. Based on your observations, what can you **infer** about the ability of sponges to move water through their bodies?

_____

_____

_____

_____

Investigate Further At one time all the sponges used by people were the skeletons of sponge animals. Today people use artificial sponges for most tasks. Use reference sources to find out what artificial sponges are made of and why people use these sponges instead of natural sponges.

_____

_____

_____

Name _____

Date _____

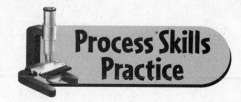
Infer

Observe the butterfly and moth below. How do these two insects differ?
What can you infer about them, based on their coloring?

_____

_____

_____

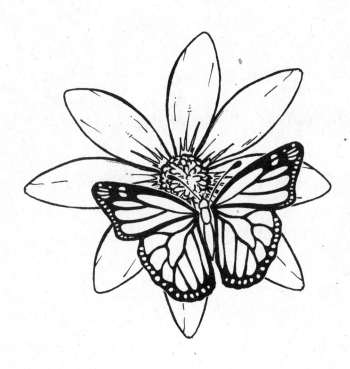

Arrange Events in Sequence

Read the paragraph below. Then fill in the blanks with numbers to put the events in sequence to show how a sponge takes in food.

    A sponge is an animal with a bag-shaped body that lives in water. The sides and bottom of this "bag" are made up of two layers of cells with a jellylike material between them. Like a bag, the top of a sponge is open. A sponge has many small openings called pores. Water enters a sponge through these pores. As this water moves through the cells on the inside of the sponge, tiny "whips" on these cells remove food from the water. The water then leaves the sponge through the opening at the top.

_____ Inside the sponge, "whips" on the cells take food from the water.

_____ The pores of the sponge are open.

_____ Water leaves the sponge through an opening at the top.

_____ Water enters the pores.

Concept Review

What Are Animals?

Lesson Concept

Animals range from simple creatures such as sponges and worms to large, complex animals with many body parts. Animals can be classified by their body structure. Two large groups are classified by whether the animals have backbones.

Use the following vocabulary terms to complete each sentence below.

Vocabulary

arthropods (A16)   **invertebrate** (A16)   **vertebrate** (A16)

1. An animal with a backbone is known as a _____.

2. Most animals do not have backbones. They are called

   _____ animals.

3. _____ are the largest group of invertebrates.

4. Explain how worms and sponges are alike and different.

   _____

   _____

   _____

   _____

Name _____

Date _____

Cones and Fruits

Materials

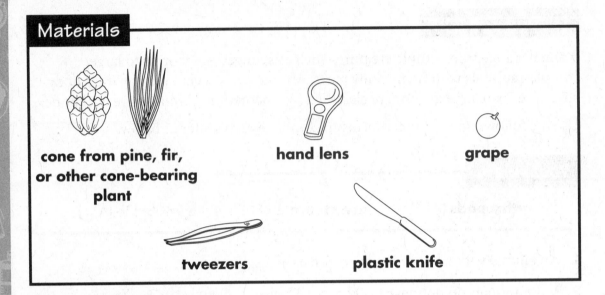

cone from pine, fir, or other cone-bearing plant

hand lens

grape

tweezers

plastic knife

Activity Procedure

1. **Observe** the cone and the grape. Describe how each looks, feels, and smells. **Record** your observations.

2. Now **observe** the cone and the grape more closely with a hand lens. Be sure to look closely at and between the scales of the cone. **Record** your observations.

3. The seeds in a cone are located between the cone's scales. Use your fingers to widen the space between several scales of the cone as much as possible. Then use the tweezers to remove the seeds from between the scales. See Picture A on page A19.

4. **Observe** the seeds with the hand lens and **record** your observations.

5. Use the plastic knife to cut the grape in half. Look for the seeds of the grape. **Record** your observations. See Picture B on page A19.

6. Use the tweezers to remove the seeds from the grape. **Observe** the seeds with the hand lens and **record** your observations. Be sure to wash your hands after handling the pine cone and grape.

Draw Conclusions

1. Both cones and fruits contain seeds. **Compare** the cone and fruit you observed in this activity.

_____

_____

2. Compare the shapes of the seeds from the cone and the grape.

_____

_____

3. Scientists at Work Scientists **compare** objects by using what they have **observed** about each object. Scientists have observed that when mature, the scales of a cone spread apart, allowing the seeds to fall from the cone. When a fruit matures, the entire fruit, along with its seeds, drops from a plant. Use this observation to **compare** the roles of cones and fruits.

_____

_____

_____

Investigate Further Obtain several other types of fruit. Cut each fruit open to **observe** its seeds. Make a table in which to **classify** the seeds you observe according to their shapes.

_____

_____

Observe and Compare

The seeds of some fruits look different, depending on how the fruit is cut.
Carefully slice an apple in half from pole to pole. Draw below left what you see.
Now slice another apple in half around the equator. Draw in the space below right
what you see. Observe the different appearance of the seeds.

Apple, pole-to-pole slice	Apple, equator slice

Compare the two, using your drawings to help you notice how they are different.
What do you notice?

_____

_____

_____

_____

Arrange Events in Sequence

Read the paragraphs below. Then write numbers in the blanks to put in sequence the events of flowers forming seeds.

Most plants you are familiar with form seeds in flowers. Flowers are reproductive structures. The male part of a flower forms pollen. The female part forms eggs.

As in cone-bearing plants, seeds form in a flower after part of a pollen grain and an egg join. As the seed forms, the part of the flower holding the seed changes and becomes a fruit. A fruit is the part of a flowering plant that contains and protects seeds.

_____ The seeds form and grow.

_____ Pollen parts and egg cells join.

_____ Fruit grows around each seed to protect it.

_____ Male parts of the flower form pollen. Female parts of the flower form egg cells.

Name _____

Date _____

**Concept Review**

What Are Plants with Seeds?

Lesson Concept

The plant part from which a new plant grows is called a seed. Cone-bearing plants have uncovered seeds. Flowering plants have fruit that covers and protects each seed.

Use the following vocabulary terms to complete each sentence below.

Vocabulary

embryo (A20)   **flower** (A22)   **fruit** (A22)

1. The part of a flowering plant that contains and protects the seed is the

_____.

2. A young plant, called an _____, encloses a cell to give it shape.

3. Describe how the cones of cycads and fir trees differ.

_____

_____

_____

_____

Name _____

Date _____

Observing Spore Prints

Materials

two kinds of
mushrooms

hand lens

white paper

Activity Procedure

1 Obtain two different kinds of mushrooms. **Observe** all the parts of each mushroom, and make a drawing of what you see.

2 Carefully separate the cap of each mushroom from the stalk.

3 Write your name at the bottom of a clean sheet of white paper. Then place the paper on a flat surface as directed by your teacher. Place each of your mushroom caps on the paper so the tops face up. See Picture A on page A25.

4 Without moving the mushroom caps, trace around the outside edge of each cap with a pencil. Be sure to wash your hands after handling the mushrooms.

5 Allow the mushrooms to remain undisturbed overnight.

6 Gently lift and remove each mushroom cap from the paper. **Observe** the pattern left on the paper. Draw and **record** your observations.

7 The pattern beneath each mushroom cap is formed by spores. **Observe** the spores with a hand lens. Draw and describe what you observe. Be sure to wash your hands after handling the mushrooms. **CAUTION** Dispose of the caps and spores as your teacher tells you. See Picture B on page A25.

Name _____

Investigate Log

Draw Conclusions

1. **Compare** and **contrast** the mushrooms you observed.

   _____

   _____

   _____

2. Describe the patterns formed by the spores.

   _____

   _____

3. **Scientists at Work** Scientists **infer** what happens in nature by making careful observations. Based on what you **observed** in the investigation, what can you **infer** about where the spores of mushrooms are formed?

   _____

   _____

   _____

   Investigate Further Do you think other mushrooms will make spore prints like the ones you just observed? **Form a hypothesis** about mushrooms and spore prints. Then **plan and conduct an experiment** to test your hypothesis.

   _____

   _____

   _____

   _____

Observe and Infer

Choose a piece of fruit or a vegetable, and carefully cut it in half. Roll one half firmly on a hard surface, deliberately bruising it. Place both pieces of fruit in a plastic bag and close the bag. Observe the fruit over the next week. What do you observe about the growth of mold? What can you infer, based on your observations?

_____

_____

_____

_____

_____

_____

_____

_____

_____

_____

_____

Use with page A25.

Name _____

Date _____

Compare and Contrast

Read the paragraphs below. Then use the Venn diagram below to show how molds and yeasts are alike and different.

Molds are common fungi that look like cotton or wool. Some molds, such as *Penicillium*, is used in making medicine. Some cheeses have molds in them. When molds form on bread or vegetables, the food has spoiled.

Another common fungus is yeast. Yeast is a single-celled fungus. It is used in the baking of bread. Some people get sick from certain kinds of yeast.

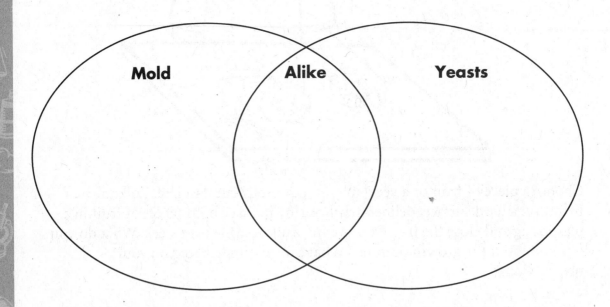

Mold   Alike   Yeasts

Use with page A27.

What Are Fungi?

Lesson Concept

Fungi include mushrooms, molds, yeasts, and mildews. They cannot make their own food. The cells of fungi have cell walls like plant cells. Fungi and algae may live together and form lichens.

Use the following vocabulary terms to complete each sentence below.

Vocabulary

fungi (A26)	**spore** (A27)
hyphae (A27)	**mold** (A28)

1. A _____ is a cell that can become a new fungus.

2. Single-celled or many-celled living things that cannot make their own food

are called _____.

3. A type of fungus that appears woolly or cottony is known as a _____.

4. The threadlike, densely packed parts of mushrooms are called _____.

5. Why do scientists now classify fungi as a separate group of organisms, instead of with plants?

_____

_____

_____

_____

Recognize Vocabulary

Use the terms below to complete the sentences. The page numbers in ( ) tell you where to look in the chapter if you need help.

Vocabulary	
cells (A6)	**vertebrate** (A16)
cell wall (A8)	**embryo** (A20)
chloroplast (A8)	**fruit** (A22)
microorganisms (A9)	**fungi** (A26)
arthropods (A16)	**mold** (A28)

Living things are made up of _____. Plant cells have

a _____ and _____, which

animal cells do not have. _____ are made up of one or a

few cells and are too small to be seen without a microscope.

Scientists classify animals according to whether the animal has a backbone.

A _____ is an animal with a backbone. The largest

group of animals that do not have backbones is known as

_____.

A young plant, or _____, makes up part of a seed.

The seeds in flowering plants are protected by the

_____.

_____ are single-celled or many-celled living things

that cannot make their own food. A cottony or woolly fungus is called a

_____.

Compare and Contrast Animals

Informative Writing—Compare and Contast

Write a paragraph that will help a younger child tell the difference between a worm and a snail. Tell how these two animals are alike and how they are different. Use the Venn diagram below to help you organize your writing.

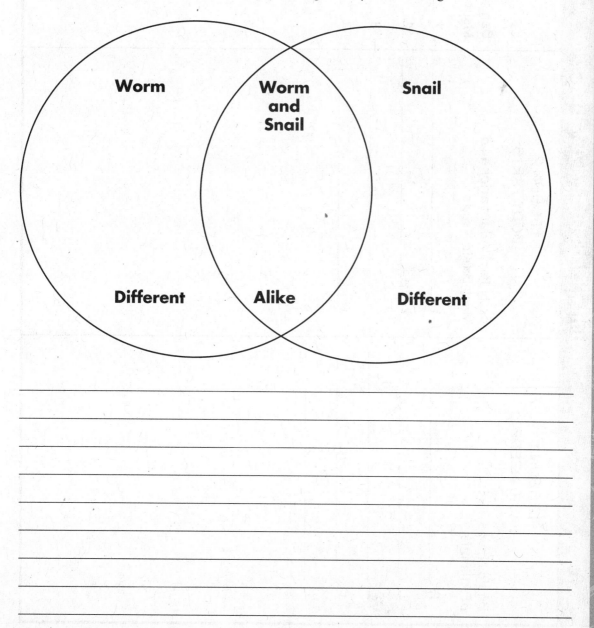

Worm

Worm
and
Snail

Snail

Different

Alike

Different

_____

_____

_____

_____

_____

_____

_____

_____

_____

Chapter 2 • Graphic Organizer for Chapter Concepts

Animal Growth and Adaptations

LESSON 1
BASIC NEEDS

Basic Needs
of Animals

1. _____

2. _____

3. _____

4. _____

5. _____

LESSON 2
BODY PARTS

Body Part Adaptations to
Meet Basic Needs

1. _____

2. _____

3. _____

4. _____

LESSON 3
BEHAVIORS

Behavior Adaptations to
Meet Basic Needs

1. _____

2. _____

3. _____

4. _____

Name _____

Date _____

Basic Needs of Mealworms

Materials

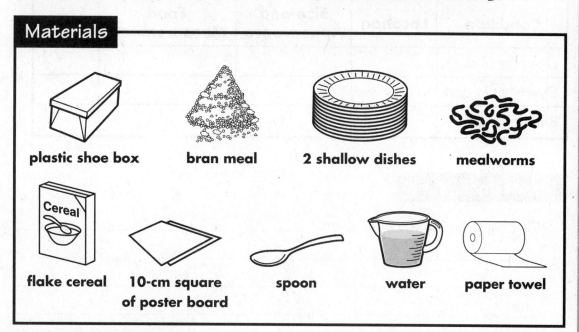

plastic shoe box   bran meal   2 shallow dishes   mealworms

flake cereal   10-cm square of poster board   spoon   water   paper towel

Activity Procedure

1. Use the chart on the next page to **record** your observations and measurements.

2. **Measure** two spoonfuls of bran meal. Put them into a shallow dish. Put it at one end of the shoe box. Count 20 flakes of cereal. Put them into another shallow dish. Put this dish at the other end of the shoe box. Fold the paper towel into a square. Moisten it and put it in the center of the shoe box.

3. Fold about 1 cm down on opposite sides of the poster board. It should stand up like a small table. Put it over the paper towel.

4. Put the mealworms in the shoe box next to, but NOT on, the towel. Put the lid on the box. Then put the shoe box in a dark place for an hour. Be careful not to spill anything.

5. Take the box to a dimly lit area. Open the lid, and **observe** the contents. Try to find the mealworms. **Record** your observations. Put the lid back on.

6. Put the box in a dark place overnight. Again, take the box to a dimly lit area. **Observe** the contents of the box. **Record** your observations. **Measure** the bran meal and count the cereal flakes. Record your measurements.

7. Put the box into bright sunshine for a few minutes. Does anything change? What can you **infer** from the location of the mealworms?

Name _____

Investigate Log

Mealworm Observations				
Condition	**Location**	**Size and Appearance**	**Food Measurements**	**Other**
One hour in dark				
Overnight in dark				
Bright sunlight				

Draw Conclusions

1. What happened to the mealworms? _____

_____

_____

2. What happened to the food? _____

_____

Why? _____

_____

3. Scientists at Work Scientists learn by **observing**. What can you **infer** about animal needs by observing the mealworms? _____

_____

_____

_____

Investigate Further How could you find out which food the mealworms liked best? **Plan an investigation.** Decide what hypothesis you would like to test and what procedure you will follow. _____

_____

_____

_____

Observe and Infer

Observing is using your senses to notice details around you. An inference is a possible explanation of something you observed.

Think About Observing and Inferring

Arthur enjoys watching the gray squirrels that scamper through his neighborhood. He decided to make a chart to record his observations of the squirrels. On his chart he also made inferences about how the squirrels were meeting their needs.

Observations of Squirrels	Inferences About Needs
Squirrel runs up a tree close to the top and goes into leafy nest.	Squirrel uses the nest for shelter.
Squirrel opens a horse chestnut, takes a bite, and throws it away.	Squirrel is looking for good food to eat.
Squirrel jumps on birdbath and lowers its head near the water.	Squirrel is bathing its face and its paws.
Squirrel eats a sunflower seed under a birdfeeder.	Squirrel has found food it likes.
Squirrel carries a twig to the top of a tree and goes into its nest.	Squirrel wants to play a game with its babies.

1. What inference might Arthur make about the squirrel's diet?

_____

_____

_____

2. Evaluate Arthur's other inferences. Which observations would you consider

   good evidence for or against each of these inferences? _____

_____

_____

_____

_____

_____

_____

Compare and Contrast

Plants and Animals: Alike and Different

At first glance, you may consider plants and animals very different life forms with no similarities at all. In fact, plants and animals have both similarities and differences.

Most animals have a short growth pattern that finishes with adulthood. Plants, however, continue to grow throughout their lives. Plants obtain their energy through photosynthesis. Animals get their energy by consuming food that they have obtained, sometimes from plants. Animals and plants are both multicelled organisms. The cells of animals are surrounded by a plasma membrane, while the cells of plants are surrounded by a wall of cellulose and a membrane. The cells of both plants and animals contain organelles. A nervous system in animals allows them to respond to their environments with movements unavailable to plants.

Complete the chart below by filling in ways in which plants and animals are alike and different.

Plants and Animals	
Compare	**Contrast**

Use with page A42.

Name _____

Date _____

What Are the Basic Needs of Animals?

Lesson Concept

All animals have common basic needs.

Vocabulary

environment (A40)   **climate** (A41)   **oxygen** (A41)

shelter (A43)   **metamorphosis** (A44)

Fill in the blank with the correct vocabulary term. Use the words in the list above.

1. Everything that surrounds and affects a living thing is called its

   _____.

2. Some insects molt, form a chrysalis around their bodies, and change from larvae to adults. This process of changing body shape is called

   _____.

List the needs all animals have by filling in the diagram below. For each of the needs, write an example of how one animal fulfills that need. The first one has been done as an example.

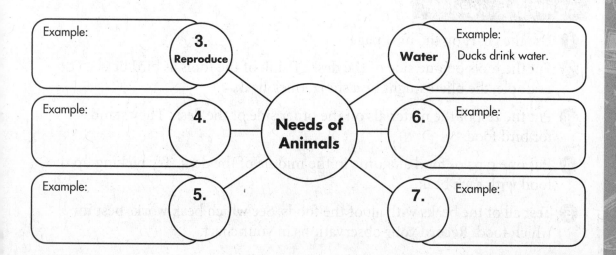

Example:

3. Reproduce

Example:

4.

Needs of Animals

Example:

Water

Example: Ducks drink water.

6.

Example:

Example:

5.

7.

Example:

Name _____

Date _____

Bird Beaks and Food

Materials

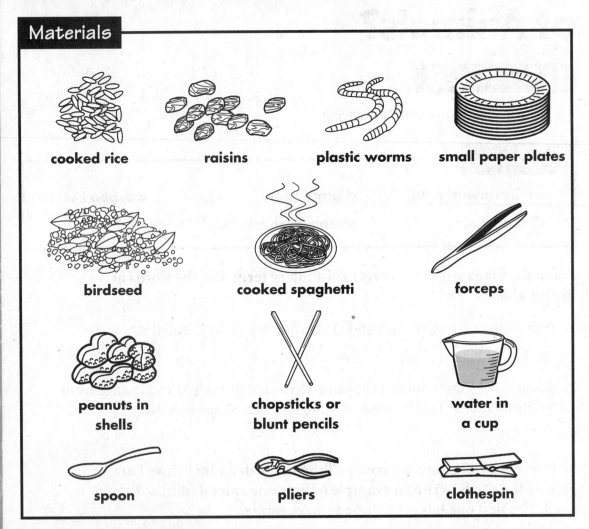

cooked rice   raisins   plastic worms   small paper plates

birdseed   cooked spaghetti   forceps

peanuts in shells   chopsticks or blunt pencils   water in a cup

spoon   pliers   clothespin

Activity Procedure

1. Use the chart on the next page.

2. Put the tools on one side of the desk. Think of the tools as bird beaks. For example, the pliers might be a short, thick beak.

3. Put the rest of the materials on the other side of the desk. They stand for bird foods.

4. Put one type of food at a time in the middle of the desk. Try picking up the food with each beak.

5. **Test** all of the beaks with all of the foods. See which beak works best for which food. **Record** your observations in your chart.

Name _____

Bird-Food and Beak Observations

Food	Best Tool (Beak)	Observations
plastic worms		
cooked spaghetti		
cooked rice		
raisins		
birdseed		
peanuts in shells		
water		

Draw Conclusions

1. Which kind of beak is best for picking up each food? _____

_____

_____

_____

Which is best for crushing seeds? _____

_____

2. By **observing** the shape of a bird's beak, what can you **infer** about the food the

bird eats? _____

_____

3. Scientists at Work Scientists often **use models** to help them test ideas. How

did using models help you test ideas about bird beaks? _____

_____

_____

Investigate Further Find a book about birds. Identify real birds that have beaks
like the tools you used in this investigation. Make a booklet describing each beak
type and how birds use it to gather and eat food. Include your own pictures of the
beaks and of the matching foods each beak can best gather and eat.

Use a Model

Books have pictures of different animals with unusual adaptations.
You can make and use models of these adaptations to learn more
about how they help animals meet their needs.

Think About Making and Using Models

Malcolm read in a book that the toucan's beak was large but very light. Malcolm
wondered how the bird used its large beak. He decided to make a model of the
toucan's beak. He cut a wide cardboard tube in half lengthwise and hinged the two
halves together with paper fasteners. He made cuts in the ends of the tube to make
a curved point. He cut jagged edges in the model to look like a toucan's beak.

Malcolm used his model to try to pick up the foods listed on the chart. The
chart shows his results.

Food	How Toucan Beak Model Performed
Plastic insects	OK; hard to grab with tip because hard
Plastic worms	OK; easier to grab because soft
Blueberries	Good; easy to grab because soft and larger than raisins
Whole peach	Very good; easy to grab because soft and large
Peanuts in shell	OK; hard to grab because hard
Birdseed	Poor; seeds too small to pick up with beak

1. What conclusions could Malcolm draw from his results? _____

_____

_____

2. How was Malcolm's model like a real toucan beak? _____

_____

3. How was it different? _____

_____

_____

4. How could Malcolm evaluate whether or not his model gave him good results?

_____

Use Context Clues to Determine/Confirm Word Meaning

Read the selection below for information on bats. Then use the context to determine the meanings of the boldfaced words. Check a dictionary to confirm your ideas.

Batty About Bats

It is safe to say that most people are not eager to spend any time with a bat. Yet bats are fascinating animals that use their unique characteristics to adapt to their environments.

Despite the phrase "blind as a bat," some bats have excellent vision. Those bats that do not have good vision make up for it by using their highly specialized sense of **echolocation**. Bats emit ultrasonic clicks. When these clicks bounce back off solid objects, the bats are alerted to the presence of the objects.

Bats are also the only mammals that fly. All other "flying" mammals are actually gliders. When bats sleep, they hang upside down so that they are in the best position for flying should danger approach. Bats are extremely beneficial **predators**. The average bat can consume as many as 650 mosquitoes each night, in addition to other insects!

Highlighted Term	What It Might Mean	What It Does Mean
echolocation		
predators		

Name _____

Date _____

How Do Animals' Body Parts Help Them Meet Their Needs?

Lesson Concept

Animals have adaptations, which enable them to meet their needs.

Vocabulary

adaptation (A48)   **camouflage** (A52)   **mimicry** (A52)

The ptarmigan (TAR•mih•guhn) is a white bird that lives in the harsh environment near the tops of mountains and also in the Arctic. It eats leaves and mosses and lichens that grow on rocks. Study the picture of the ptarmigan, and write about how each of the body parts listed below is an adaptation that helps the ptarmigan meet its needs. Use at least one of the vocabulary terms.

Feathers _____

_____

Color _____

_____

Feet _____

_____

Bones _____

_____

Beak _____

_____

Use with page A53.

Name _____

Date _____

Monarch Butterfly Travel

Materials

outline map of North America

2 pencils of different colors

Activity Procedure

1 Label the directions north, south, east, and west on your map.

2 During the summer many monarch butterflies live in two general areas. Some live in the northeastern United States and around the shores of the Great Lakes. Others live along the southwestern coast of Canada and in the states of Washington and Oregon. Locate these two large general areas on your map. Shade each area a different color.

3 At summer's end large groups of monarchs gather and travel south for the winter. Most of those east of the Rocky Mountains fly to the mountains of central Mexico. But some of these butterflies make their way to Florida. Butterflies west of the Rocky Mountains fly to sites along the California coast. All of these areas have trees where the butterflies can rest, temperatures that are cool yet above freezing, and water to drink. Find these areas on your map. Shade each winter area the same color as the matching summer area. Then use the right color to draw the most direct route from north to south over land.

Name _____

Draw Conclusions

1. **Compare** the climate where the monarch butterflies spend the summer with the climate where they spend the winter. _____

   _____

   _____

2. What can you **infer** about how the behavior of the butterflies helps them meet their needs? _____

   _____

   _____

3. **Scientists at Work** Scientists use maps and graphs to **communicate** data and ideas visually. How does making a map of butterfly movements help you understand where monarchs travel? _____

   _____

   _____

   _____

Investigate Further Many kinds of birds, fish, and mammals travel to different places when the seasons change. Research the travel route of one of these animals. Use a map to show the route.

My animal: _____

Where it travels: _____

_____

Why it travels: _____

_____

Name _____

Date _____

Communicate

When you communicate, you give information to someone. You can use words or a map or both to communicate information about animal migration.

Think About Communicating

Read the information about the migration routes and schedules of some North American birds. Use pencils of different colors to trace the path that each type of bird follows on its migration.

The common tern winters along the coast of southern Florida. It flies north, reaching the southern edge of the Great Lakes by May 1. It reaches its summer range in central-western Canada by June 1.

The short-eared owl winters everywhere in the United States. Some owls migrate north into Canada for the summer. They reach central Canada by May 1. Those that fly all the way to the Arctic arrive by June 1.

The ruby-throated hummingbird winters in central Mexico. These birds all migrate to the eastern half of the United States for the summer. Some stay in the south. Others continue migrating north. Those that migrate north reach the Smoky Mountains by April 1 and an area just south of the Great Lakes by May 1.

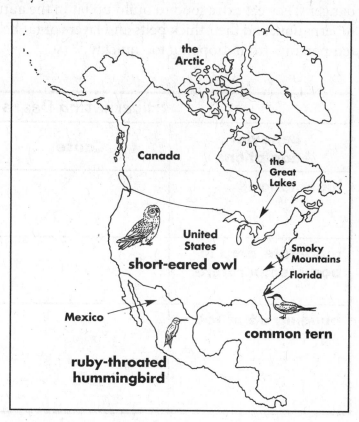

Of the two forms of communication used here, the words and the map, which

gave you the most information the most quickly? Explain. _____

_____

_____

_____

Identify Cause and Effect

Read the selection. Then complete the chart by supplying a cause and effect for each of the bear's behavior adaptations.

The Adaptable Bear

Bears are animals that adapt well to the environment by adjusting their behavior. Bears around the world hibernate in winter months because there is less food available. Their hibernation differs from that of other mammals that hibernate, such as chipmunks or ground squirrels, because their body temperature does not drop as drastically. The body temperature of bears stays within 12°F (11°C) of their normal temperature, allowing them to wake and react quickly to danger. They eat extra food to build up fat in the autumn to nourish them during hibernation, and their thick pelts and layers of fat help keep their body temperature from dropping too quickly.

Hibernating Bears		
Behavior Adaptations	**Cause**	**Effect**
hibernation		
moderate drop in body temperature		
building up of fat		

How Do Animals' Behaviors Help Them Meet Their Needs?

Lesson Concept

Animals behave in ways that enable them to meet their needs. The behaviors are adaptations to their environments.

Vocabulary

instinct (A56)   **migration** (A57)   **hibernation** (A59)

1. For each behavior, write **I** if it is an instinct or **L** if it is a learned behavior.

_____ Atlantic green turtles migrate to Ascension Island.

_____ Ground squirrels hibernate during the winter.

_____ Mother tigers hunt for food.

_____ You read this worksheet.

_____ Pacific salmon return to the stream where they hatched.

_____ Chimpanzees call to one another.

2. How could a scientist determine if a behavior is an instinct or is learned?

_____

_____

_____

3. Many places are very cold during the winter. If an animal does not have adaptations to live through the cold winter, what two things could it do to survive until the spring? What must the animal have to do these things?

_____

_____

_____

_____

Name _____

Date _____

Recognize Vocabulary

Use the terms below to fill in the word puzzle.

environment	climate	oxygen	shelter
metamorphosis	adaptation	camouflage	mimicry
instinct	migration	hibernation	

Across

3. helps an animal blend with its surroundings

5. a behavior an animal is born with

7. changes made from an egg to a larva to an adult

9. the movement from one region to another and back again

10. a body part or behavior that helps an animal meet its needs

Down

1. everything that surrounds and affects an animal

2. a long, deep "sleep"

3. average temperature and rainfall

4. an animal looks much like another animal

6. a place where an animal can protect itself

8. a gas in the air animals need

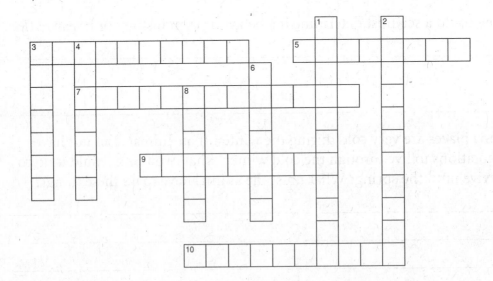

Use with pages A38–A61.

Name _____

Date _____

Write a Poem About Animal Homes

Expressive Writing–Poem

Write a poem about the ways different animals find shelter. Use the word web to help you plan your writing. Start the lines of your poem with the letters of the word SHELTER. Use the lines provided to help you plan your poem.

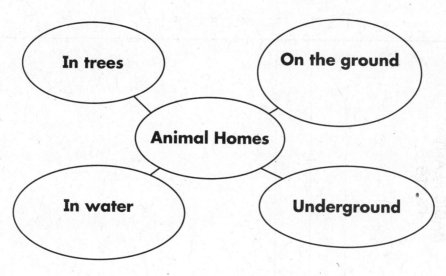

S _____

H _____

E _____

L _____

T _____

E _____

R _____

Name _____ Date _____

Plant Growth and Adaptations

LESSON 1
BASIC NEEDS OF PLANTS

Needs

1. _____

2. _____

3. _____

4. _____

LESSON 2
BASIC PLANT PARTS

Parts

1. _____

2. _____

3. _____

LESSON 3
WAYS PLANTS REPRODUCE

Way   Example

1. _____

2. _____

3. _____

4. _____

5. _____

6. _____

Parts for Reproduction

1. _____

2. _____

3. _____

4. _____

How Light Affects Plants

Materials

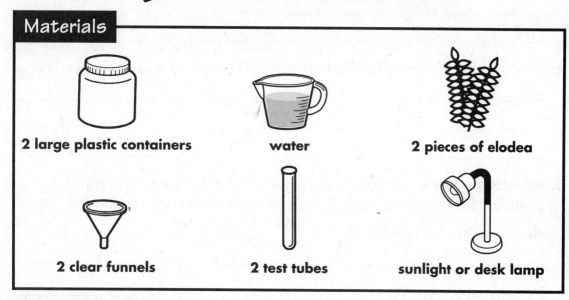

2 large plastic containers   water   2 pieces of elodea

2 clear funnels   2 test tubes   sunlight or desk lamp

Activity Procedure

1. Fill one container about $\frac{2}{3}$ full of water. Place one piece of elodea in the water.

2. Turn a funnel wide side down, and place it in the water over the elodea. There should be enough water in the container so that the small end of the funnel is just below the water.

3. Fill a test tube with water. Cover the end with your thumb and turn the tube upside down. Place the test tube over the end of the funnel. Allow as little water as possible to escape from the tube.

4. Repeat Steps 1–3 using the second container, funnel, piece of elodea, and test tube.

5. Set one container of elodea in sunlight or under a desk lamp. Set the other in a dark place, such as a closet.

6. After several hours, **observe** the contents of each container.

Name _____

Draw Conclusions

1. **Compare** the two test tubes. What do you **observe**? _____

   _____

   _____

2. One test tube is now partly filled with a gas. What can you **infer** about where

   the gas came from? _____

   _____

   _____

3. **Scientists at Work** Scientists **control variables** to learn what effect each
   condition has on the outcome of an experiment. What one variable did you

   change in this investigation? _____

   _____

   What variables were the same in both containers? _____

   _____

   _____

Investigate Further How fast can a plant make oxygen? Repeat the procedure
for the plant placed in light, but use a graduate instead of a test tube. **Measure** the
amount of oxygen in the graduate every 15 minutes for 2 hours. **Record** your
findings. Make a line graph to show how fast the plant produced oxygen.

Name _____

Date _____

Identify and Control Variables

Identifying and controlling variables helps you set up an investigation. These results may show you what you want to find out. For your investigation to work, you need to change one variable related to what you want to know. You keep all the other variables the same.

Think About Identifying and Controlling Variables

Raphael read that plants get nutrients from the soil. He wanted to check this information by doing an experiment. He took two plants of the same type and size and planted one in a pot containing small plastic plant pellets and the other in a pot containing the same amount of potting soil. He put the plants next to each other in a sunny window and watered them with equal amounts of water every three days. Every week he observed the plants closely, measured their growth, and recorded his observations. The picture shows a page from Raphael's observation journal after the second month of the experiment.

October 25: Day 60

Plant in soil

Observations: After two months, the plant in the soil had grown 2 inches. It was green and healthy looking. The stem was firm. The leaves were shiny. The plant had several new, young leaves. The plant in the plastic pellets, however, had not grown and showed no signs

1. Which variables did Raphael control in this experiment?

_____

_____

2. What did Raphael vary and why? _____

_____

3. Compare the two plants. Do you think Raphael's results gave evidence that

plants get nutrients from the soil? Explain. _____

_____

Arrange Events in Sequence

Read the selection below. Then number the blanks in the order in which the statements appear in the selection.

Round and Round We Go

One of nature's most delicate cycles is the carbon–oxygen cycle. Living things, such as plants and animals, depend on these two gases.

The cycle begins for plants as they absorb carbon dioxide from the air. They then use carbon dioxide during photosynthesis, giving off oxygen as a result. Animals use oxygen and give off carbon dioxide each time they breathe out. Decomposers, such as fungi and bacteria, use oxygen and produce carbon dioxide as they break down animal waste, dead animals, and plants as food. Carbon dioxide and oxygen move through the atmosphere. Throughout this trading of gases, the amounts of these two gases in the atmosphere usually stay about the same.

_____ Decomposers use oxygen and produce carbon dioxide.

_____ Carbon dioxide and oxygen move through the atmosphere.

_____ Plants absorb carbon dioxide from the air.

_____ Animals use oxygen and give off carbon dioxide when they breathe out.

_____ The balance of oxygen and carbon dioxide remains the same.

Use with page A73.

What Do Plants Need to Live?

Lesson Concept

Plants have adaptations to help them meet their needs.

Vocabulary

carbon dioxide (A72)   **nutrient** (A72)   **photosynthesis** (A73)

Answer the questions below about plants.

1. List the basic needs of plants by filling in the diagram below. For each need, tell how the substance is used. Use vocabulary terms when possible.

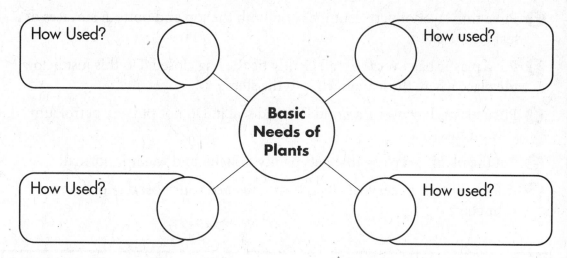

For each of the plants listed below, describe one adaptation it has and tell how the adaptation helps the plant.

2. Vine _____

_____

3. Cactus _____

_____

4. Water lily _____

_____

_____

How Plants "Breathe"

Materials

leafy potted plant   petroleum jelly   2 clear plastic bags   twist ties

Activity Procedure

1 Use the chart below.

2 Put a thin layer of petroleum jelly on both the top and bottom surfaces of a leaf on the plant.

3 Put a plastic bag over the leaf. Gently tie the bag closed. Do this just below the place where the leaf attaches to the stem.

4 Put a plastic bag over a second leaf and seal it. Do not put any petroleum jelly on this leaf.

5 Put the plant in a place that gets plenty of light, and water it normally.

6 After two days, **observe** the two leaves. **Record** your observations on your chart.

Plant Leaf	Observations
Leaf with petroleum jelly	
Leaf with no petroleum jelly	

Name _____

Draw Conclusions

1. **Compare** the two plastic bags. What do you **observe**? _____

_____

_____

_____

2. What can you **infer** from what you **observed** in this investigation?

_____

_____

_____

_____

_____

3. **Scientists at Work** Scientists often **compare** objects or events. Comparing allows the scientists to see the effects of the variables they control. Compare the leaves you used in this investigation. What can you **infer** about the effect of the

petroleum jelly? _____

_____

_____

Investigate Further Find out where gases are exchanged in a leaf. This time, coat the top side of one leaf and the bottom side of another leaf. Tie a plastic bag over

each leaf. What do you **observe**? **My observations:** _____

_____

What can you **infer**? _____

_____

_____

Name _____

Date _____

Compare

When you compare objects or events, you look for what they have in common. You also look for differences between them.

Think About Comparing

Atea knows that dandelions and irises are flowers. But they look different. She finds pictures of both these flowers. She compares them to see what is the same and what is different.

1. How are the roots of these two plants different? _____
   _____
   _____

2. How are the leaves of these two plants different? _____
   _____
   _____

3. How do you think the roots and leaves of these plants are alike? Consider what they do for the plant. _____
   _____
   _____
   _____

4. How are the stems of the two plants alike? How are they different?
   _____
   _____

Summarize and Paraphrase a Selection

Read the passage below. Then fill in the table with the appropriate characteristic and role of each plant part.

Breaking All the Rules

Water lilies grow in both warm and hot climates. They are known for their large, nearly round leaves and for their brightly colored flowers. The scent of the flowers attracts insects for pollination. After pollination, the stems draw the flowers back under water. Seeds develop and are released under water.

Water lily roots grow down into the soil beneath lakes and ponds. The roots draw nutrients from the soil and anchor the plants. A long stem grows up to the leaves, which float on the surface of the water. A tube in the stem carries oxygen to the roots. If the water level rises, stems grow to keep leaves at the surface.

Functions of the Water Lily's Parts		
Plant Part	**Characteristics**	**Role of This Plant Part**
Leaves		
Stems		
Roots		

Use with page A79.

How Do Leaves, Stems, and Roots Help Plants Live?

Lesson Concept

Plants have leaf, stem, and root adaptations that help them meet their needs. Some plants have parts that trap and digest insects to get needed nutrients.

Vocabulary

dormancy (A78)   **transpiration** (A78)   **taproot** (A79)   **fibrous root** (A79)

Write the letter of the best answer to each question on the line.

1. The two main leaf types are

   _____.

   A broad leaves and needle leaves
   B flat leaves and needle leaves
   C broad leaves and spines

2. The main functions of most leaves

   are to _____.

   A take in moisture and give off gases
   B take in moisture and give support
   C carry on photosynthesis and exchange gases

3. The main functions of most stems

   are to _____.

   A carry on photosynthesis
   B support plants and give them shape
   C protect plants and store food

4. Compared with fibrous roots, a

   taproot is _____.

   A thin and grows near the surface of the soil
   B thick and grows deep into the soil
   C long, with branching root hairs growing from it

5. Meat-eating plants trap insects

   because _____.

   A they cannot make their own food
   B they cannot absorb enough sunlight
   C their soil lacks enough nutrients

6. Transpiration occurs in a plant when

   _____.

   A the leaves trap an insect
   B the leaves give off water
   C the roots give off water

Seedling Growth

Materials

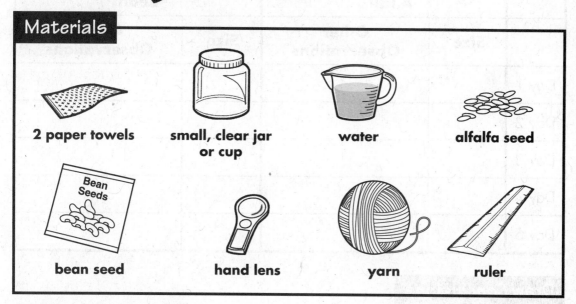

2 paper towels   small, clear jar or cup   water   alfalfa seed

bean seed   hand lens   yarn   ruler

Activity Procedure

1. Fold the paper towel, and place it around the inside of the jar.

2. Make a second paper towel into a ball, and place it inside the jar to fill the space.

3. Place the alfalfa seed about 3 cm from the top of the jar, between the paper-towel lining and the jar's side. You should be able to see the seed through the jar.

4. Place the bean seed in a similar position on the other side of the jar.

5. Pour water into the jar to soak the towels completely.

6. Set the jar in a warm place, and leave it there for five days. Be sure to keep the paper towels moist.

7. Use the chart on the next page.

8. Use the hand lens to **observe** the seeds daily for five days. **Measure** the growth of the roots and shoots with the yarn. Use the ruler to measure the yarn. **Record** your observations on your chart.

Name _____

Seed Growth				
	Alfalfa		**Bean**	
	Size	**Other Observations**	**Size**	**Other Observations**
Day 1				
Day 2				
Day 3				
Day 4				
Day 5				

Draw Conclusions

1. What plant parts grew from each seed? _____

_____

2. Compare the growth of the roots and the shoots from the two seeds. Did they

grow to be the same size? _____

_____

_____

Did they grow at the same rate? _____

_____

_____

3. Scientists at Work Scientists take a lot of care to **measure** objects the same
way each time. Think about how you measured the plants. How do you know

your measurements were accurate? _____

_____

_____

Investigate Further The bean and alfalfa seedlings will continue to grow after
the first five days. Plant each of the seedlings in soil. Then **plan and conduct an
experiment** to find out whether alfalfa or beans grow better in dry conditions. You
will probably need to use three or more seedlings of each type.

Name _____

Date _____

Measure

Measuring is a way to observe and compare objects and events accurately. When you measure, you may want to use an instrument, such as a ruler, a balance, or a stopwatch.

Think About Measuring

A group of students wanted to find out how much food three different kinds of corn plants would produce. They formed two teams. Each team grew ten plants of each kind of corn. When the plants were grown, they harvested the corn. To figure out how much food each type of corn produced, both teams removed all the ears of corn from the stalks. They removed the husks from around the corn. Team 1 cut the corn kernels from the cob and used a balance to find the mass of the corn kernels. Team 2 measured the mass of whole ears of corn. The following table shows both teams' results.

Corn Produced			
Team	Corn A	Corn B	Corn C
1	5 kg	2.5 kg	2 kg
2	10 kg	8 kg	6.5 kg

1. Could the teams get the answer to their question about which types of corn produced the most food based on their results? Explain your answer.

   _____

   _____

2. Whose method of measuring how much food each kind of corn plant produced was most accurate, Team 1's or Team 2's? Explain your answer.

   _____

3. If the students had just counted the number of ears produced by each plant type, would they come to the same conclusions?

   _____

   _____

Reading Skills Practice

Use Context Clues to Determine/Confirm Word Meanings

Read the selection on conifers. Then use context clues to help you determine or confirm word meanings. Remember that some clues are in the form of examples.

Conifers

Conifers are the largest group of gymnosperms, or nonflowering seed plants. Some examples of conifers are pines, spruces, and firs. Most members of this group of gymnosperms produce both male and female cones on the same tree. The pollen from the male cones depends on the wind for pollination of the female seed cones. Most conifers have needlelike or scalelike leaves. Many, but not all, conifers are evergreens.

Conifers are among the oldest forms of trees known. Conifer fossils have been found to be as old as 300 million years! Some conifers are among the world's tallest trees. Examples of tall conifers are the coastal redwoods in northern California, Douglas firs, and cypresses. Other conifers are known for their long lives. Redwoods and bristlecones are two examples of long-living conifers. They have been known to live for 3,500 years and longer!

Gymnosperms	
Tall conifers	
Long-living conifers	

How Do Plants Reproduce?

Lesson Concept

Plants reproduce in many ways.

Vocabulary

germinate (A84)	**stamen** (A85)	**spore** (A85)
pistil (A85)	**pollination** (A85)	**tuber** (A87)

Tell how the seed in each picture would be most likely to spread.

1. _____

_____

_____

_____

2. _____

_____

_____

_____

3. How are spores different from seeds? _____

_____

_____

_____

4. Describe four ways people can grow new plants without planting seeds.

_____

_____

_____

_____

Recognize Vocabulary

Read the following sentences. On each line, write the letter for the
word or words that best go with the underlined words.

carbon dioxide	**nutrient**	**photosynthesis**	**dormancy**
transpiration	**taproot**	**fibrous root**	**germinate**
spore **tuber**	**pistil**	**stamen**	**pollination**

_____ 1. To make food, plants need <u>gas breathed out by animals.</u>

      A carbon dioxide   **B** nutrients   **C** spore

_____ 2. Trapping sunlight to make food energy is <u>the process that makes food
in a plant.</u>

      A pollination   **B** germination   **C** photosynthesis

_____ 3. Grass is a plant that has <u>many roots of the same size.</u>

      A taproots   **B** tubers   **C** fibrous roots

_____ 4. A seed <u>sprouts</u> when its need for water, air, and warmth is met.

      A tubers   **B** germinates   **C** spores

_____ 5. Plants can lose water through <u>the process in which water is given off
by plant parts.</u>

      A transpiration   **B** dormancy   **C** photosynthesis

_____ 6. Broad-leafed trees drop their leaves when they enter <u>a period without
growth.</u>

      A photosynthesis   **B** dormancy   **C** transpiration

_____ 7. Soil provides plants with <u>substances needed for growth.</u>

      A carbon dioxide   **B** nutrients   **C** pistils

_____ 8. Some plants form <u>tiny cells</u> to make new plants.

      A tubers   **B** nutrients   **C** spores

_____ 9. <u>Swollen underground stems</u> can be used to make new plants.

      A tubers   **B** nutrients   **C** stamens

_____ 10. Dandelions have <u>one main root that goes deep into the soil.</u>

      A fibrous roots   **B** tubers   **C** taproots

Writing Practice

Write a Speech

Persuasive Writing—Advocacy

Imagine that your community is making plans to clear wooded land that is home to many birds and insects. Write a speech you could give to your zoning board, urging the community to protect the habitat. Support your position with information about the role of birds and insects in pollinating and germinating plants. Use the outline below to help you plan your speech.

State your opinion:
State reasons: **Reason 1:**
Reason 2:
Reason 3:
Restate your opinion or call for action:

Chapter 4 • Graphic Organizer for Chapter Concepts

Human Body Systems

LESSON 1
SKELETAL SYSTEM

What It Does

_____
_____

Main Parts

1. _____
2. _____

MUSCULAR SYSTEM

What It Does

_____
_____

Main Parts

1. _____
2. _____
3. _____

LESSON 2
RESPIRATORY SYSTEM

What It Does

_____
_____

Main Part

1. _____

CIRCULATORY SYSTEM

What It Does

_____
_____

Main Parts

1. _____
2. _____
3. _____
4. _____

LESSON 3
NERVOUS SYSTEM

What It Does

_____
_____

Main Parts

1. _____
2. _____
3. _____
4. _____

DIGESTIVE SYSTEM

What It Does

_____
_____

Main Parts

1. _____
2. _____
3. _____
4. _____

Muscle Tissues

Materials

Slide A—skeletal muscle tissue

Slide B—smooth muscle tissue

Slide C—heart muscle tissue

Microslide Viewer

Activity Procedure

1. Use the chart below.

2. Use the Microslide Viewer to carefully **observe** the muscle tissue on microslide 1 or the picture of Slide A on page A96.

3. Take notes to describe the way the tissue looks. What shapes do you see? Are there any colors or patterns?

4. **Record** your observations on your chart as notes or sketches.

5. Repeat Steps 2–4 for microslides 2 and 3, or Slides B and C on page A96.

Type of Muscle	Observations	Ways Like Other Types of Muscle	Ways Different from Other Types of Muscles
Slide A			
Slide B			
Slide C			

Name _____

Investigate Log

Draw Conclusions

1. Describe each type of muscle tissue.

   Slide A _____

   _____

   Slide B _____

   _____

   Slide C _____

   _____

2. How do the tissues look the same? _____

   _____

   How do they look different? _____

   _____

   _____

   _____

3. **Scientists at Work** Many scientists use microscopes in their work. What does a microscope do that makes it possible to **observe** and **compare** muscle tissues?

   _____

   _____

   _____

   _____

Investigate Further If you have access to a microscope, use one to **observe** prepared slides of different kinds of tissue. See page R3 for help in using a microscope. Cells from different kinds of tissue in your body look different. Find pictures of other kinds of tissue, such as nerve tissue, bone tissue, and blood tissue. **Compare** these tissues with the muscle tissues you looked at.

Name _____

Date _____

Observe and Compare

Looking at something closely is one way of observing. You extend your sense of sight when you use a hand lens or a microscope. As you make observations, you may compare the different things you observe.

Think About Comparing

Your blood is made up of a variety of different cells floating in a watery fluid. Study the diagrams of different types of blood cells, as they would appear stained and under a microscope. Then answer the questions.

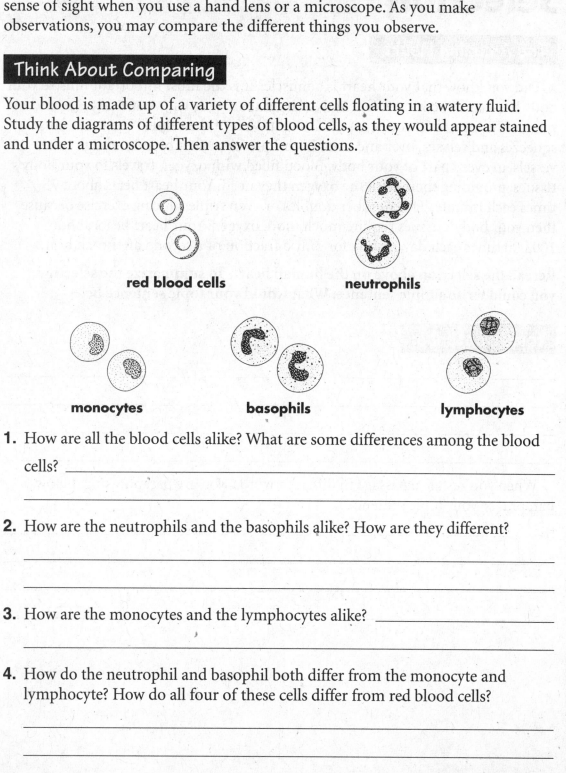

red blood cells   neutrophils

monocytes   basophils   lymphocytes

1. How are all the blood cells alike? What are some differences among the blood cells? _____

   _____

2. How are the neutrophils and the basophils alike? How are they different?

   _____

   _____

3. How are the monocytes and the lymphocytes alike? _____

   _____

4. How do the neutrophil and basophil both differ from the monocyte and lymphocyte? How do all four of these cells differ from red blood cells?

   _____

   _____

Use with page A97.

Summarize and Paraphrase a Selection

The Amazing Heart

Did you know that your heart is a muscle? It is the most important muscle your body has—and the most efficient. No larger than your fist, your heart is a kind of pump. It is located in your chest, just slightly left of the center. The heart muscle squeezes and relaxes, over and over. Each squeeze pushes blood through tubes, or vessels, to every part of your body. Blood filled with oxygen travels to your body's tissues, providing them with the oxygen they need. Your heart beats about 75 times each minute. This number doubles or even triples during exercise because then your body's tissues require much more oxygen. Your heart beats about 100,000 times each day, resting for only a fraction of a second after each beat.

Reread the selection above on the human heart. To summarize the selection, you could write a topic sentence. What would your topic sentence be?

Topic Sentence:

_____

_____

_____

_____

When you restate a passage in different words, you are paraphrasing. Below, paraphrase your topic sentence.

_____

_____

_____

_____

Concept Review

How Do the Skeletal and Muscular Systems Work?

Lesson Concept

The skeletal and muscular systems work together to help the body move.

Vocabulary

tissue (A98)	organ (A98)	cardiac muscle (A99)
smooth muscle (A99)	striated muscle (A100)	

Fill in the diagram to describe the basic parts that make up your body.

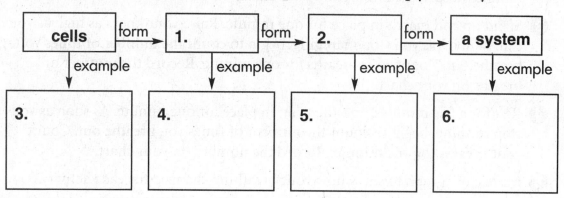

| cells | →form→ | 1. | →form→ | 2. | →form→ | a system |

example ↓   example ↓   example ↓   example ↓

3.   4.   5.   6.

List four functions of your skeletal system.

7. _____ _____

_____ _____

Identify each type of muscle tissue, and tell where it is in the body.

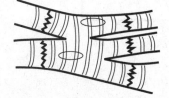 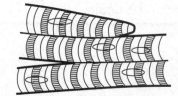 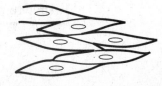

8. _____   9. _____   10. _____

_____   _____   _____

_____   _____   _____

Breathing Rates

Materials

stopwatch, timer, or clock with second hand

Activity Procedure

1. Use the chart below.

2. While you are sitting, count the number of times you breathe out in one minute. **Record** the number on your chart.

3. Stand up and march in place for one minute. Raise your knees as high as you can. As soon as you stop marching, begin to count the number of times you breathe out. Count your breaths for one minute. **Record** the number of breaths on your chart.

4. Rest for a few minutes, and then run in place for one minute. As soon as you stop running, begin to count the number of times you breathe out. Count your breaths for one minute. **Record** the number on your chart.

5. Make a bar graph to show how your breathing changed for each activity.

Activity	Number of Breaths
Sitting	
After marching for 1 minute	
After running for 1 minute	

Investigate Log

Draw Conclusions

1. Which activity needed the fewest breaths? _____

   Which needed the most breaths? _____

2. What can you **infer** about breathing from what happened in this investigation?

   _____

   _____

   _____

3. **Scientists at Work** Scientists don't usually **measure** something just once. What could you do to be sure your breathing rate measurements were correct?

   _____

   _____

   _____

Investigate Further Does your breathing rate increase if you exercise longer? **Form a hypothesis** about breathing and length of exercise. Then **plan and conduct an experiment** to test your hypothesis. You may want to build on what you have done already in this Investigate. For example, march in place for two minutes, and then count your breaths. Run in place for two minutes, and then count your breaths.

Activity	Number of Breaths
Sitting	
After marching for 1 minute	
After running for 1 minute	
After marching for 2 minutes	
After running for 2 minutes	

Name _____

Date _____

Measure

When you make observations that involve numbers, usually you are measuring. You can use an instrument, such as a ruler, a stopwatch, or the device shown below, to make measurements.

Think About Measuring

Taylor was interested in finding out how much air people can hold in their lungs. She looked in a science book and found instructions for making a device that measures how much air people can breathe out. She made the device, called a spirometer (spy•RAH•muh•ter) as shown. She used the device to measure how much air her classmates could breathe out in one breath. Her results are listed on the chart. (Air volume is measured in cubic centimeters.)

Subject	Amount of Air Breathed Out
Melissa	1400 cc
Jordan	1500 cc
Sam	1700 cc
Charlotte	1500 cc
Latasha	1400 cc
Paul	600 cc
Ricardo	1200 cc
Patricia	1300 cc
Rita	1400 cc
Robbie	1600 cc
Ms. Bell	2100 cc

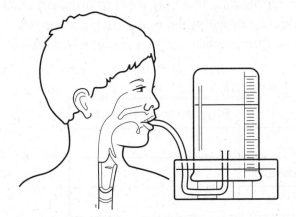

1. What was Taylor measuring and how did she make her measurements?

_____

2. Taylor thought that some of her measurements might be wrong. Which measurements do you think she might be worried about? Why?

_____

_____

3. What do you think Taylor should do about the possible faulty measurements?

_____

_____

Compare and Contrast

The Blood's Circular Trip

The human heart alone is not enough to make the circulatory system work. Thousands of miles of hollow tubes called blood vessels carry the blood through the body, to and from the heart.

Blood vessels called arteries carry blood away from the heart. The blood that has passed through the lungs is filled with oxygen, which the arteries deliver to all the cells of the body. Arteries branch out in the body until they form very small tubes. These very small tubes are called capillaries. Capillaries connect the arteries to other blood vessels called veins.

Veins carry blood toward the heart. Unlike arteries, veins have valves on the inside that prevent the blood from flowing backward, much like gates that allow traffic to move in only one direction.

Both veins and arteries have three layers: an outer layer of tissue, a middle layer of smooth muscle, and a smooth lining of cells.

If all the blood vessels in an average child were laid out in a line, the line would be over 60,000 miles long!

Reread the selection above. Then write sentences that compare and contrast veins and arteries.

Compare

_____

_____

_____

_____

Contrast

_____

_____

_____

_____

Name _____

Date _____

How Do the Respiratory and Circulatory Systems Work?

Lesson Concept

The respiratory and circulatory systems deliver oxygen to the body and remove wastes.

Vocabulary

lungs (A104)   **capillary** (A104)   **heart** (A105)   **artery** (A105)   **vein** (A105)

Answer the questions below.

1. What happens in the lung's air sacs, shown at the right?

   _____

   _____

   _____

   _____

   _____

2. List in order the types of blood vessels blood travels through as it goes from the heart to the body cells and back again. What happens in the blood vessels near the body cells? _____

   _____

   _____

3. How do your heart and lungs work together to carry out their main functions?

   _____

   _____

   _____

   _____

   _____

The Sense of Touch

Materials

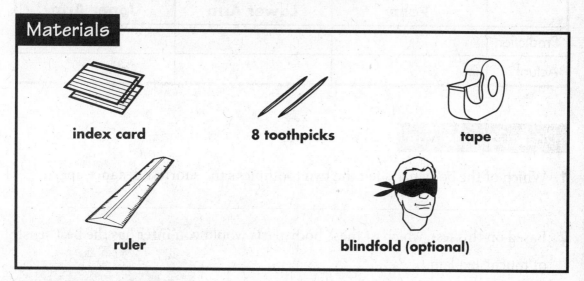

index card   **8 toothpicks**   **tape**

ruler   **blindfold (optional)**

Activity Procedure

1 Use the chart on the next page.

2 Look at the areas of the body listed on the chart. **Predict** which one has the best sense of touch. Write your prediction on the chart. Explain your choice.

3 Measure a space 1 cm wide on one edge of the index card. Mark each end of the space, and write the distance between the marks. Tape a toothpick to each mark so that one end of each toothpick sticks out about 1 cm past the edge of the card. Make sure the toothpicks point straight out from the edge of the card.

4 Repeat Step 3 for the other three sides of the index card. However, use spaces 2 cm, 5 cm, and 8 cm wide, one for each side.

5 Have a partner test your sense of touch. Ask him or her to lightly touch one body area listed on the chart with the toothpicks on each edge of the index card. Begin with the 1-cm side, then use each side in turn with spaces 2 cm apart, 5 cm apart, and 8 cm apart. Don't watch as your partner does this.

6 For each area, tell your partner when you first feel two separate toothpicks touching your skin. Have your partner write the distance between these toothpicks on the chart.

7 Switch roles and test your partner.

Name _____

Distance Between Toothpicks When Two Toothpicks First Felt			
	Palm	**Lower Arm**	**Upper Arm**
Prediction			
Actual			

Draw Conclusions

1. Which of the body parts felt the two toothpicks the shortest distance apart?

_____

2. Based on this test, which of these body parts would you **infer** has the best sense of touch? Explain. _____

_____

3. Scientists at Work Using what you observed in this investigation, which part of your body do you **predict** to be more sensitive, your fingertip or the back of your neck? _____

Investigate Further Have your partner use the toothpicks to test your fingertip and the back of your neck to check the **prediction** you just made.

My observations: _____

_____

_____

Predict

Predicting involves telling what you think will happen in the future. You make predictions based on observations you have made before or experiences you have had in the past.

Think About Predicting

Mr. Brown's class was learning about how the nervous system works. They learned that with practice, they could increase how fast they could send messages from their brains to their muscles. This is called improving reaction time.

The class decided to do an experiment to see if practicing to music could help them improve their reaction time even more than practice without music would. The class formed one large circle, with all the students holding hands. Two students near the teacher broke hands, so that these students were holding the hand of only one other student. Mr. Brown gave one of these students a stopwatch. When Mr. Brown said, "Go," the student with the stopwatch started it running; the other student squeezed the hand of the student next to him or her. As soon as that student felt the squeeze, he or she would squeeze the hand of the next student. When the student holding the stopwatch felt the squeeze, he or she stopped the timer and announced the class reaction time. The class did the next trial with slow music and the third trial with fast music. They did eight of each kind of trial in sequence, as described.

Reaction Time:		
No Music	**Slow Music**	**Fast Music**
28 seconds	28 seconds	27 seconds
27 seconds	26 seconds	24 seconds
25 seconds	24 seconds	24 seconds
24 seconds	24 seconds	25 seconds
22 seconds	22 seconds	21 seconds
23 seconds	22 seconds	19 seconds
22 seconds	23 seconds	17 seconds
21 seconds	22 seconds	16 seconds

1. Based on these results, how could the class improve their reaction time even more? On what observations or experience do you base this prediction?

_____

_____

_____

_____

_____

Arrange Events in Sequence

How Do Nerve Cells Communicate?

Have you ever wondered how your brain gets messages to the rest of your body or how it receives messages from other parts of your body? For instance, what happens when you touch something hot? Your brain and nervous system go into gear. Together they tell you in less than a second to remove your hand from the hot object.

The sequence of events starts with your hand. When you touch the hot object, sensory nerves in the skin send electrical impulses along nerves that run like wires up your arm, to your spine, and up to your brain. Nerve cells are called neurons. The message is passed between neurons by the movement of chemicals called neurotransmitters. Neurotransmitters flow from a message-sending neuron across a gap called a synapse. They attach to a slot, called a receptor site, on the surface of the receiving neuron.

Once the impulse reaches the spinal cord, it is identified as very urgent. The spinal cord sends the electrical message two ways. One set of messages returns down the arm to lift the hand from the hot object. The other message goes to your brain to tell you that the pain you are feeling in your hand is a burn.

The words below are taken from the selection above. Use some of these words to write a paragraph that describes, in the correct sequence, the events that take place in your nervous system when you burn your hand.

| impulses | neurotransmitters | neurons | brain |
| spinal cord | receptor site | synapse | |

_____

_____

_____

_____

_____

_____

_____

Concept Review

How Do the Nervous and Digestive Systems Work?

Lesson Concept

The brain controls the way all other body systems work. The digestive system breaks down food to provide nutrients for all the body's cells.

Vocabulary

brain (A110)	**neuron** (A110)	**nerve** (A110)
spinal cord (A110)	**esophagus** (A112)	**stomach** (A112)
small intestine (A112)	**large intestine** (A113)	

Answer the questions below.

1. What does your nervous system do? _____

_____

Organ	What Happens
2. _____	**3.** _____
4. _____	**5.** _____
6. _____	**7.** _____
8. _____	**9.** _____
10. _____	**11.** _____

Name _____

Date _____

Recognize Vocabulary

In the space provided, write the letter of the term in Column B that best fits the definition in Column A.

Column A

_____ 1. This blood vessel carries blood away from the heart.

_____ 2. This muscle makes up the heart.

_____ 3. Connects nerves in your body to your brain

_____ 4. Type of muscle found in the walls of your organs

_____ 5. This blood vessel carries blood to the heart.

_____ 6. The control center of your nervous system

_____ 7. This kind of blood vessel is the smallest.

_____ 8. This is formed from tissues of different kinds working together.

_____ 9. These organs take oxygen into your body.

_____ 10. This kind of tissue makes up the muscles in your arms and legs.

_____ 11. This organ pumps blood throughout your body.

_____ 12. Water is removed from digested food here.

_____ 13. Food is liquified in this organ.

_____ 14. Food is digested the most here and taken into the body.

_____ 15. These connect the sense organs in your head to your brain.

_____ 16. Cells of the same type form this.

_____ 17. These cells are the basic unit of the nervous system.

_____ 18. Tube that goes from your mouth to your stomach

Column B

A vein

B brain

C organ

D cardiac muscle

E spinal cord

F esophagus

G nerves

H stomach

I small intestine

J neurons

K large intestine

L tissue

M smooth muscle

N capillary

O striated muscle

P lungs

Q heart

R artery

Use with pages A96–A113.

Name _____

Date _____

Informative Writing

Write a Health Pamphlet

Write a pamphlet telling children how to maintain good cardiovascular health. Include at least four tips. Use references to find resources on heart and lung health to recommend in your pamphlet. Recommend one printed resource and one multimedia or Internet resource. The outline below will help you organize your writing.

How to Maintain Good Cardiovascular Health

Tip 1:
Tip 2:
Tip 3:
Tip 4:
Recommended resources:

Chapter 1 • Graphic Organizer for Chapter Concepts

Ecosystems

LESSON 1 SYSTEMS

Definition _____

_____

Types of Systems

1. _____

2. _____

Examples of Systems

1. _____

2. _____

LESSON 2 ECOSYSTEMS

Definition _____

_____

Groups of Organisms in Ecosystems

1. _____

2. _____

Nonliving Parts of Ecosystems

1. _____ 2. _____

3. _____ 4. _____

5. _____

LESSON 3 HABITATS AND NICHES

Habitat _____

_____

Niche _____

Types of Roles

1. _____

2. _____

3. _____

LESSON 4 TROPICAL RAIN FORESTS AND CORAL REEFS

Tropical Rain Forest _____

_____

Rain Forest Homes

1. _____ 2. _____

Coral Reef _____

_____

Coral Reef Homes _____

_____

LESSON 5 OCEAN COMMUNITIES

Near-shore zone— _____

Open-ocean zone— _____

Intertidal zone— _____

Name _____

Date _____

How Parts of a System Interact

Materials

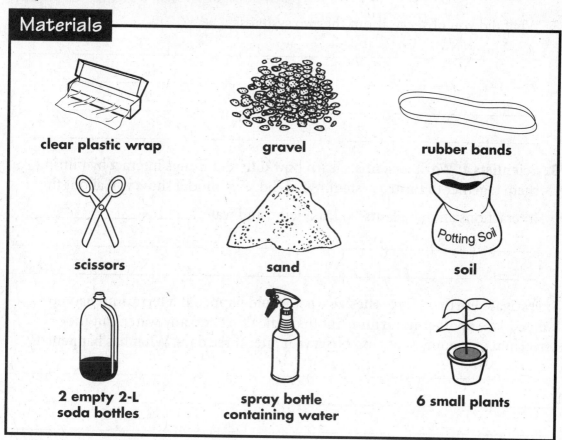

clear plastic wrap   gravel   rubber bands

scissors   sand   soil

2 empty 2-L   spray bottle   6 small plants
soda bottles   containing water

CAUTION

Activity Procedure

1 **CAUTION** **Be careful when using scissors.** Cut the tops off the 2-L bottles.

2 Pour a layer of gravel in the bottom of each bottle. Cover this with a layer of sand.

3 Add a layer of soil to each bottle, and plant three plants in each bottle.

4 Spray the plants and the soil with water. Cover the tops of the bottles with plastic wrap. You may need to use the rubber bands to hold the plastic wrap in place. You have now made two examples of a system called a *terrarium* (tuh•RAIR•ee•uhm).

5 Put one terrarium in a sunny spot. Put the other in a dark closet or cabinet.

6 After three days, **observe** each terrarium and **record** what you see.

Name _____

Draw Conclusions

1. Which part of the system was missing from one of the terrariums?

_____

_____

2. What did you **observe** about the two systems? _____

_____

_____

_____

_____

3. Scientists at Work Scientists learn how different things interact by putting them together to form a system. What did your **model** show you about the interactions among plants, soil, air, light, and water? _____

_____

_____

Investigate Further Hypothesize what would happen if a terrarium had no water. Make another terrarium, but this time don't add any water. Put the terrarium in a sunny spot, and **observe** it after three days. What has happened?

_____

_____

_____

_____

Name _____

Date _____

Make a Model

In nature, systems tend to be complex. Making a model of a natural system can help you see how specific parts of that system interact.

Think About Making a Model

Cheryl has two similar aquariums. These aquariums are the same size. Each holds four goldfish and three small aquarium plants. Cheryl decided to use one aquarium to model a sunny pond. She put it near a window that received several hours of direct sunlight daily. She put one aquarium away from windows, so it got no direct sunlight. She observed the two aquariums for a month. She recorded her observations.

Date	Aquarium in Direct Sunlight	Aquarium Not in Direct Sunlight
Nov. 5	Fish stay in shadows of plants when sun shines directly on tank.	Fish swim throughout tank.
Nov. 15	Glass is beginning to look green. Fish still avoid sun.	Aquarium glass is clear. Fish swim throughout tank.
Nov. 25	Glass has green streaks, especially where sunlight strikes glass. Fish swim throughout tank.	Glass is clear. Fish swim throughout tank.
Dec. 5	Glass is greener than before. Gravel and water are beginning to look green. Fish swim throughout tank.	Aquarium glass and water are clear. Fish swim throughout tank.

1. What are the parts common to both aquarium systems? _____

   _____

   Which part was missing from one of the aquariums? _____

2. What was the main difference Cheryl observed between the two aquariums?

   _____

   _____

3. What do these models show you about the interactions among the fish, plants,

   water, gravel, and sunlight? _____

   _____

Identify Cause and Effect

Read the paragraph. Then complete the chart to show some of the causes and effects found in the water cycle.

The Rain Cycle

About three-fourths of Earth's surface is covered with water. The water cycle begins when the sun heats ocean water. Some of the ocean water evaporates and travels through the atmosphere in the form of water vapor. A cloud forms high in the atmosphere where the temperatures are much colder. This colder temperature causes the water vapor to condense and form water droplets. As the water droplets in the clouds join together, they get larger and heavier. Eventually the heavy raindrops fall to Earth in the form of rain. The rainwater collects in lakes, rivers, and oceans, and on land. Some of the rain that falls on land sinks deep into the ground. We call this groundwater.

Parts	Cause	Effect

For Review

...ystems?

...ems, have different parts that interact.

stability (B8)

...stem. Describe this system by filling in the chart.

System Parts	Examples
Living parts	
Nonliving parts	
Inputs	
Outputs	
Patterns of short-term change	
Long-term stability	

Name _____

Date _____

An Ecosystem

Materials

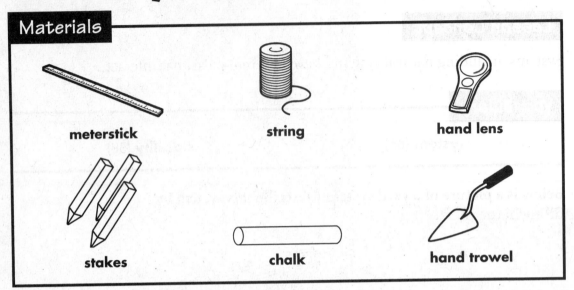

meterstick

string

hand lens

stakes

chalk

hand trowel

Activity Procedure

1 Use the meterstick to **measure** a square area that is 1 m long and 1 m wide. It can be on grass, bare dirt, or the cracked concrete of a wall or sidewalk. Mark the edges of the square with the chalk or with the stakes and string.

2 **Observe** your study area. Look for plants and animals that live there. Use the hand lens. **Record** all the living things you see. Describe any signs that other living things have been there.

3 *In soil or grass,* use the trowel to turn over a small area of soil. Look for insects or other living things. **Count** and **record** any living things you find. Then **classify** them. Be sure to fill in the holes you dig in your area.

4 *In concrete or brick areas,* **observe** areas along the sides of the concrete or bricks that may contain soil and places for plants to grow. **Count** and **record** the number of each type of living thing you find. Then **classify** each.

5 **Communicate** your results to your class. Describe your study area. Identify the living things you found.

Name _____

Draw Conclusions

1. What living things did you find in your study area? _____

_____

_____

Which kind of living thing was most common in your area?

_____

_____

_____

2. How was your study area different from those of other student groups?

_____

_____

_____

3. Scientists at Work Scientists often **observe** an ecosystem at different times of the day and in different seasons. This is because different animals can be seen at different times. **Predict** the different animals you might see if you observed your study area at different times of the day or at different times of the year.

_____

_____

_____

_____

Investigate Further Choose an area that is like the area you **observed.** Repeat the investigation. What was the same? _____

_____

What was different? _____

_____

Why were there differences? _____

_____

_____

Name _____

Date _____

Observe

Observing includes using all of your senses to notice things around you.

Think About Observing

Raj knew that ecosystems like his backyard change from day to night. He wondered what this ecosystem was like at night. Raj decided to observe this ecosystem. He took a flashlight, a pencil, and a notebook and went out in his backyard after dark. He heard sounds right away. He heard the wind blowing through the leaves, a dog barking, crickets chirping, and rustling in the raspberry patch.

Raj took his flashlight and quietly walked over to investigate the raspberry patch. He turned the flashlight on. Staring back at him was a family of raccoons. He slowly backed away from the raspberry patch so the mother raccoon wouldn't be startled.

Raj slapped at the mosquitoes buzzing and trying to bite him. He looked up at the sky. The stars were shining. He heard a bird call out and saw it soaring high overhead. He thought he saw other birds flying, too, in a swooping, fluttery flight. He tried to shine his flashlight on them. But they were too dark and moved too fast for him to see well.

1. What were the different animals Raj observed? _____
_____

2. What senses did Raj rely on to make his observations? _____
_____

3. Which sense do you think was most important in making these observations? Explain your answer. _____
_____
_____
_____

4. Soon after Raj saw the bird, he had to go back inside. If he wanted to check in the morning for signs of nighttime activity, what do you think he should look for? _____
_____
_____

Identify the Main Idea and Supporting Details

Read the selection below. Then identify the main idea and all of the supporting details.

Desert Life

Many plants and animals have adapted well to the harsh conditions of the desert. Some of these plants and animals could not survive in other climates and ecosystems. Although desert conditions can be harsh, the desert is home to a large variety of plants and animals.

Plants survive the desert conditions by adaptations to the severe conditions. Some plants survive the dry conditions by having seeds that lie dormant for long periods of time, waiting to bloom again when the rains return. Succulents (SUHK•yoo•luhnts), such as the American cactus and the African euphorbia (YOO•for•bee•uh), adapt by storing water.

Many animals live well in desert conditions. Among these animals are insects, reptiles, mammals, and birds. They depend on the plants for food, shelter, and protection from other animals. The animals, in turn, help the plants survive by carrying seeds from place to place and by pollinating the plants.

Main Idea

Supporting Details

What Makes Up an Ecosystem?

Lesson Concept

An ecosystem is made up of groups of living things and their environment.

Vocabulary

ecosystem (B12)   population (B13)   community (B14)

Write the letter of the best answer on the line.

1. An ecosystem is made up of different species of living things _____.
   A called a population   **C** and the environment
   B called an estuary   **D** and sunlight

2. In an ecosystem all living things _____.
   A have unusual adaptations   **C** grow quickly
   B grow slowly   **D** can meet their basic needs

3. All ecosystems contain populations of different organisms; a population is a
   group of _____.
   A the same species living in the same place at the same time
   B the same species living in the same place throughout the species' history
   C different species living in the same place at the same time

4. Mangrove trees are adapted to live in an ecosystem where _____.
   A water is scarce   **C** there is very deep water
   B saltiness of the water varies widely   **D** clarity of the water varies widely

5. Ecosystems contain communities, in which _____.
   A different populations compete for limited resources
   B different populations depend on one another for survival
   C organisms of a single population compete with each other for resources

6. The important nonliving parts of an ecosystem include air, water, soil, _____.
   A sunlight, and temperature   **C** heat, and carbon
   B salt, and sunlight   **D** shade, and bacteria

The Homes and Roles of Living Things

Materials

index cards

reference books about animals

crayons or markers

Activity Procedure

1. Each member of your group should choose five different animals.

2. Draw a picture of each of your animals on a separate index card.

3. Using five more cards, draw the homes of your animals or show them in their roles. Look up information about your animals in reference books if you need help.

4. Gather all the cards. Mix up the cards, and place them face down. Take turns playing Concentration®. Turn over two cards at a time until you find a pair that shows an animal and its home or role. Explain how the two cards match. Play until all the matches have been made.

Name _____

Draw Conclusions

1. What new animals did you learn about as you played the game?

   _____

   _____

   _____

   _____

2. Which was easier to identify, an animal's home or its role? Explain your answer.

   _____

   _____

   _____

   _____

3. **Scientists at Work** Scientists often make **inferences** based on things they have **observed** and their past experiences. What inferences did you make as you tried to explain how two cards matched? _____

   _____

   _____

   _____

   _____

Investigate Further Choose an animal card, and think of another animal that may have the same home or role. Suppose the new animal meets its needs in the same community. **Form a hypothesis** about how it will interact with the other animals. Will they try to eat the same food or use the same places for shelter? Will the new animal keep the animal on the card from meeting its needs? Use library resources to test your hypothesis.

   _____

   _____

   _____

   _____

   _____

   _____

   _____

Name _____

Date _____

Observe and Infer

Inferring involves explaining something based on observations you
have made and information you already know.

Think About Inferring

Below are pictures of animals and animal homes. Match the animals to their
homes. Then answer the questions about how you came up with your matches.

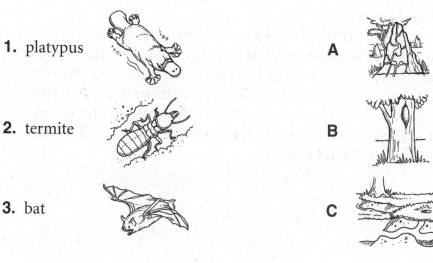

1. platypus   **A**

2. termite   **B**

3. bat   **C**

1. _____ platypus's home

How did you infer this? _____

_____

_____

_____

2. _____ termite's home

How did you infer this? _____

_____

_____

3. _____ bat's home

How did you infer this? _____

_____

_____

Use with page B19.

Arrange Events in Sequence

Read the selection below. Then use the words *first*, *next*, *then*, and *finally* to show the correct sequence of Antarctica's food chain.

Antarctica: A Unique Food Chain

You already know much about how food chains allow animals of different kinds to exist. But what about Antarctica? Did you know that most of Antarctica's living organisms are found in the water?

Millions and millions of small plantlike protists live in the ocean off the coast of Antarctica. Krill are small ocean animals that feed on the protists. Squid eat krill and other small ocean animals. The penguin is one of the most well-known Antarctic animals that comes next in the food chain. The penguin eats squid, and it has several predators. Sea birds such as gulls and terns eat fish and penguin eggs, and the leopard seal and the killer whale eat adult penguins. The killer whale is the top predator in Antarctica's food chain.

First,

_____

Next,

_____

Then,

_____

Finally,

_____

Use with page B21.

What Are Habitats and Niches?

Lesson Concept

Each living thing in an ecosystem has a habitat and a niche.

Vocabulary

habitat (B20)   **niche** (B21)   **producer** (B21)   **consumer** (B21)

decomposer (B21)   **energy pyramid** (B22)   **food web** (B23)

Read the paragraphs below about earthworms, and answer the questions that follow.

Earthworms tunnel through the soil. They eat rotting leaves and other plant parts that fall on the ground as well as the remains of small dead organisms. Their waste products, called castings, add nutrients to the soil. Earthworms dig burrows for shelter and nesting. They bring leaves from the surface down into their burrows, to line their homes.

Earthworms are food for many different animals. Birds are earthworms' main above-ground predators, as well as some kinds of turtles, frogs, toads, and snakes. Below the ground, moles are earthworms' main predators. Some people catch earthworms to use as bait for fish.

1. Describe the earthworms' habitat. _____

_____

2. List two facts about the earthworms' niche. _____

_____

_____

_____

3. What kind of animal is the earthworm—a producer, a consumer, or a decomposer? Explain your answer. Is the earthworm closer to the top or to the

bottom of the energy pyramid? _____

_____

_____

A Coral Reef

Materials

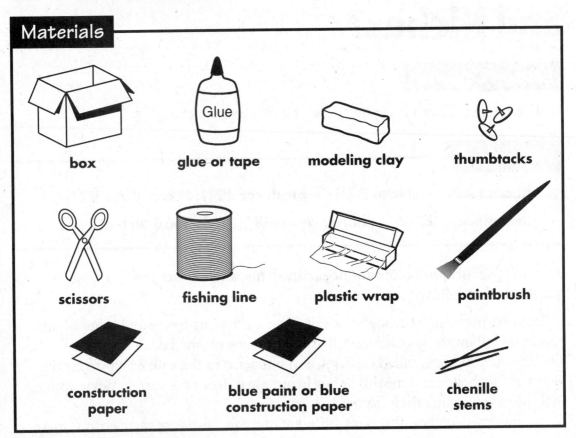

box	glue or tape	modeling clay	thumbtacks
scissors	fishing line	plastic wrap	paintbrush
construction paper	blue paint or blue construction paper		chenille stems

CAUTION

Activity Procedure

1 Look through the lesson, and use library resources to find pictures of reef organisms and their habitats.

2 Plan a diorama that uses the materials your teacher provides. Try to find the best material for each living and nonliving thing you will show.

3 Follow your plan. Keep in mind colors, sizes, and the best use of space.

4 Label the organisms in your diorama.

Name _____

Draw Conclusions

1. What organisms did you include in your diorama? _____
_____
_____
_____

2. Tell three things you learned while building your diorama.
_____
_____
_____
_____

3. **Scientists at Work** When scientists build a **model** of an organism that is very small, they may make it hundreds of times bigger. If you tried to build your diorama to scale, you may have found it hard to show the very smallest organisms. How could you show large models of the tiniest organisms and still

build your diorama to scale? _____
_____
_____
_____
_____
_____

Investigate Further A diorama can show only part of the picture. Write a paragraph or two describing other organisms that could live near your reef scene.
_____
_____
_____
_____
_____
_____
_____
_____
_____
_____

Make a Model

Models can show relationships among different organisms in an ecosystem.

Think About Making a Model

Keisha wanted to make a model of a nest of leaf-cutting ants. The ants eat fungi they grow in their gardens. These ants bite off small bits of leaves and take these leaf bits back to their underground nest. They chew up the leaf bits into a pulp and spread the pulp on their fungi garden. The green pulp makes the garden grow.

Keisha wanted to make her model larger than life-size so people could see details of the nest's structure and of the ants themselves. Leaf-cutting ants are usually less than 3 millimeters long. The leaf bits they cut may be up to four times that size.

1. If Keisha wanted to make her model in a box that measures 50 centimeters by 75 centimeters (about 20 in. × 30 in.), what do you think would be a good size to make the ants? Why would this be a good size? _____

_____

_____

2. How big should she make the leaf bits that the ants are carrying?

_____

_____

3. How could Keisha show that the nest of the leaf-cutting ants is underground?

_____

_____

4. If she wanted to show that the model is bigger than life-size, list two different things she could include in the diorama to give people looking at it a sense of

scale. _____

_____

_____

_____

_____

Reading Skills Practice

Compare and Contrast

Read the selection below. Then complete the Venn diagram by comparing and contrasting jungles and rain forests.

Is a Rain Forest a Jungle?

The terms *rain forest* and *jungle* often refer to the same type of place. Although there are similarities between the two, a rain forest and a jungle are not the same.

Jungles and rain forests both can be found in tropical climates. Jungles have very dense, bushy clumps of vegetation that grow low to the ground. Jungles can develop only when rain forests have been partially or completely destroyed by either logging or cultivation and then are abandoned. Thick, tangled vegetation grows in place of the forest trees. Rain forests are most distinguishable by their tall canopies that block much of the sun's light from ever reaching the forest floor. Only plants that require low light can grow on the floor of a rain forest. In addition, rain forests provide the world with many valuable resources, such as timber, rubber, coffee, tea, sugarcane, and bananas.

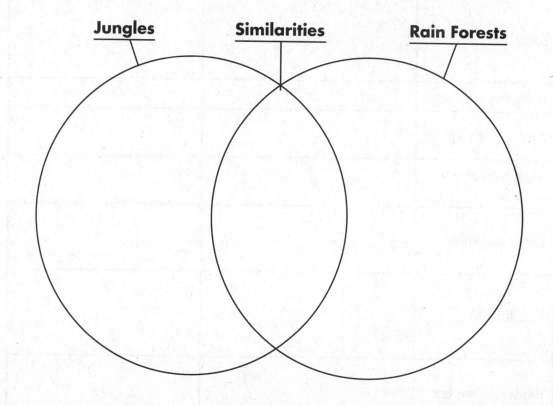

Jungles   Similarities   Rain Forests

Name _____

Date _____

 Concept Review

What Are Tropical Rain Forests and Coral Reefs?

Lesson Concept

Tropical rain forests and coral reefs are ecosystems that provide habitats to a large variety of plants and animals.

Vocabulary

climate (B28)   **diversity** (B29)   **salinity** (B30)

Fill in the chart below that compares a tropical rain forest to a coral reef.

Characteristic of Ecosystem	Tropical Rain Forest	Coral Reef
Location		
Temperature range		
Amount of sunlight		
Main type of organism		
Other organisms		
Habitats		
Resources we get from the ecosystem		

Use with page B33.

Name _____

Date _____

Investigate Salt Water and Fresh Water

Materials

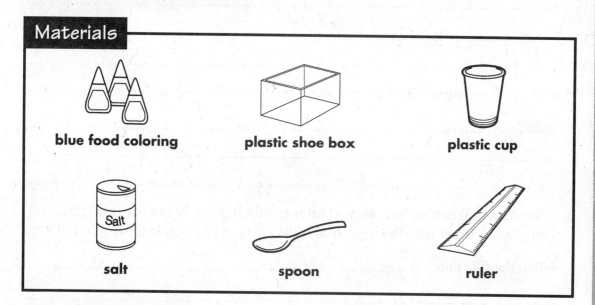

blue food coloring   plastic shoe box   plastic cup

salt   spoon   ruler

Activity Procedure

1. Put a tablespoon of salt in a cup of water and stir.

2. Add a couple drops of blue food coloring to the salt water and stir again.

3. Half-fill a plastic shoe box with fresh water.

4. Slowly and carefully pour the salt water into one end of the shoe box. Pour the salt water along the side of the shoe box so that you disturb the fresh water as little as possible. **Observe** what happens. (Picture A)

5. Blow on the water's surface to simulate wind. **Observe** what happens.

6. Dip the ruler into the water at one end of the shoe box. Slowly move the ruler up and down to simulate ocean waves. **Observe** what happens. (Picture B)

Name _____

Draw Conclusions

1. What did you **observe** when the salt water was added to the fresh water? Which is heavier, salt water or fresh water?_____

   _____

   _____

   _____

2. What did you **observe** when you made waves by blowing and by moving the ruler?_____

   _____

   _____

3. **Scientists at Work** What can you **infer** would happen when the tide rises and brings salty water into the mouth of a river? What can you **infer** would happen when the tide falls? _____

   _____

   _____

   _____

   _____

   _____

Investigate Further The area where fresh water and salt water meet and mix is called an estuary. In addition to tidal changes, the position of sea level affects where estuaries are located. Based on what you learned in this activity,

hypothesize how rising sea level would affect estuaries. _____

_____

_____

Observe and Infer

When you compare, you observe objects or events and try to find out how they are alike or different. You ask yourself questions while you are observing.

Think About Comparing and Inferring

Obtain from your teacher two samples of plants, a piece of seaweed and either a needle from a conifer or a leaf from a deciduous tree leaf. Place each of these in the salt water solution you used in the investigation. **Observe** what happens to each leaf over a few hours. What can you **infer** about the leaves, based on their reaction to salt water?

1. What happened to the seaweed after a few hours? _____

_____

2. What happened to the conifer needle or the deciduous leaf after sitting in salt

   water for a few hours? _____

   _____

3. Why did the leaves react the way they did when placed in salt water?_____

_____

_____

_____

4. What part of the solution is important to the survival of both types of plants?

_____

5. How is the seaweed different from the conifer needle or the tree leaf? _____

_____

_____

_____

Summarize and Paraphrase a Selection

Read the selection below. Then write the key points in the chart. Finally, write a paragraph that summarizes the information contained in the key points.

Kelp

Kelp, or seaweed, is found all over the world. One kind of kelp, *Laminaria*, (LAM•ih•nair•ee•uh), is found near the low-tide mark along the Pacific Coast of the United States and near the British Isles. It can grow up to 3 meters (9.8 ft) long. It absorbs the shock from ocean waves and can serve as a cushion to shorelines. Laminaria is also home to the Atlantic lobster. Laminaria is harvested for the iodine it contains.

Another type of kelp is *Macrocystis*, (MAK•roh•sis•tis). It also is called "giant kelp." It is the largest type of kelp and can grow up to 65 meters (215 ft) long. It grows along the U.S. Pacific Coast and along the coast of South America. It is home to many invertebrates and fish. It also is home to the sea otter, whose numbers were once low due to hunting. Macrocystis is harvested for a carbohydrate, algin, which is used for tire manufacturing. Algin is even added to ice cream!

Kelp

Summary:

_____

_____

_____

_____

_____

Learn About Saltwater Communities

Lesson Concept

Three different life zones make up the ocean. The *intertidal zone* is affected by high and low tides. The *near-shore zone* is shallow and can support many plants and animals. The *open-ocean zone* is the deep parts of the oceans.

Use the following vocabulary terms to complete each sentence below.

Vocabulary

near-shore zone (B36)	**water depth** (B36)	**kelp forests** (B38)
intertidal zone (B36)	**light** (B36)	**food chain** (B40)
open-ocean (B36)	**salt marshes** (B37)	**sulfides** (B40)

1. The deepest part of the ocean is in the _____ zone.

2. The _____ zone is located between the high- and low-tide zones.

3. If light can reach the ocean floor, the zone is called _____.

4. _____ and _____ determine the life zones of the ocean.

5. _____ are an example of an intertidal ecosystem.

6. _____ are similar to forests on land, except they are under water.

7. Microscopic plantlike organisms that float near the water's surface form the basis of the open ocean _____.

8. _____ form the basis of energy in deep-sea hydrothermal vents.

9. Choose one of the ecosystems discussed in the chapter and explain how plants and animals live there. _____

_____

_____

_____

Recognize Vocabulary

Use the clues to fill in the word puzzle.

Down

1. role of a living thing in its habitat
2. variety of living things
4. an organism that eats other living things
5. average temperature and rainfall over time
6. group of parts that work together
7. group of the same species living in the same place at the same time
13. diagram showing the energy flow in an ecosytem

Across

3. environment that meets the needs of an organism
6. over time changes cancel each other out
8. group of living things and the environment that they live in
9. organism that makes its own food
10. amount of salt in a liquid
11. all populations living in the same area
12. organism that feeds on the wastes or remains of living things
14. area between high- and low-tide zones
15. diagram showing how food chains overlap in an ecosystem

Name _____

Date _____

Describe a System

Informative Writing—Description

Think of a park or other natural area you like to visit. Using the outline below to help you organize, write a paragraph describing this place as a system. Illustrate your paragraph with a diagram identifying living and nonliving parts of the system. Label inputs and outputs.

Name of the park or natural area:	Diagram of system:
Living parts of the system:	
Nonliving parts of the system:	
Inputs to the system:	
Outputs from the system:	

Chapter 2 • Graphic Organizer for Chapter Concepts

Protecting Ecosystems

LESSON 1
ECOSYSTEM CHANGES

Slow Changes

1. _____

2. _____

3. _____

Rapid Changes

1. _____

2. _____

3. _____

LESSON 2
HUMAN INTERACTIONS
WITH ECOSYSTEMS

Damage Humans Cause

1. _____

2. _____

Things That Help Repair
Ecosystems

1. _____

2. _____

3. _____

LESSON 3
CONSERVING ECOSYSTEMS

Conserving Resources

1. _____

2. _____

3. _____

4. _____

Preserving Resources

1. _____

2. _____

3. _____

Changes in a Pond

Materials

aluminum foil pan   water   metric ruler

plastic green plants   aquarium gravel

Activity Procedure

1 Use the chart below. **Make a model** of a pond that has formed
in a low spot on exposed rock. Fill the pan half-full of water.

Investigation Step	Measurement of Water's Surface	Observations
Step 2		
Step 4		
Step 5		

2 **Measure** and **record** the distance across the water's surface. Try to "plant" a few plants near the sides of your pond. Record your **observations**.

3 **Predict** what will happen to the pond if you add gravel and then plants.

My predictions: _____

4 Slowly add gravel to your model pond. The gravel stands for soil that has washed into the pond during 200 years. In a real pond more soil builds up around the edges than in the middle. Put more gravel around the edges of the pond than in the middle. **Measure** and **record** the distance across the water's surface. Again "plant" several plants near the sides of the pond. Record your **observations**.

5 Add more gravel and plants until you can no longer see the water's surface. This represents several hundred years of adding soil. **Record** your **observations** of what was once a pond.

Draw Conclusions

1. Describe how your pond changed over time. _____

_____

_____

_____

2. As a pond changes, how might the living things in it change? Explain your

answer. _____

_____

_____

3. **Scientists at Work** When you **observed** your pond model, you **collected data.** What does your data tell you about how a natural pond changes over time?

_____

_____

_____

_____

Investigate Further Ponds go through *stages*, or steps, as they get older. Draw a picture showing four stages of a pond. Label the stages *new pond, old pond, marsh,* and *meadow*. The next time you visit an area outdoors, determine if any ponds are new or old. Use a drawing to record what you observe.

Name _____

Date _____

Collect Data

When you collect data, you make observations and measurements and record them in an organized way.

Think About Collecting Data

Ian lives in an area where there are many farms, meadows, and forests. He has noticed that every year certain changes occur in the countryside around him. These changes mark the seasons. Ian wants to keep track of when these seasonal changes happen in different years.

1. Ian is trying to set up an observation journal. In this journal he wants to record the dates that specific changes occur for at least the next two years. Ian also wants to record specific observations he makes on specific dates. Which of the following kinds of record books do you think would work best for Ian? Explain your answer.

 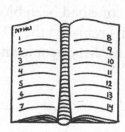 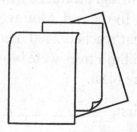

_____

_____

_____

_____

2. During the spring Ian noticed wildflowers in the woods for a few weeks. He decided to keep track of the number of different kinds of wildflowers he saw in the woods during the spring months. Describe a way he might collect this data. Tell how he could compare this data for two different years.

_____

_____

_____

_____

Arrange Events in Sequence

Read the selection. Use the words *first, next, then,* and *finally* to tell about the correct sequence of what happened at Mount St. Helens.

What happened at Mount St. Helens?

Mount St. Helens is a volcano located in the Cascade Range in southwestern Washington State. On May 18, 1980, this volcano, dormant since 1857, exploded because of a buildup of magma.

On March 27, 1980, there was a steam eruption. After moments of calm, there were more eruptions of steam. Magma rising inside the volcano caused cracks on the north side of the volcano. On May 18, an earthquake caused a landslide on the north side of the volcano and the side fell away. Soon afterward, there was an air blast that caused a cloud of hot ash to travel more than 20 kilometers (12 mi) from the summit of Mount St. Helens. River valleys east of Mount St. Helens were buried by floods, mudflows, and hot ash flows. A column rose in the sky, and gas and ash produced by the events traveled as far away as central Montana.

In the end, Mount St. Helens' cone had been blown away. A crater with rims that reached 2400 meters (7874 ft) replaced the 2950-meter (9678-ft) peak. Ten million trees were blown away, and sixty people and countless animals died in the blast.

First, _____

_____

Next, _____

_____

Then, _____

_____

Finally, _____

_____

What Kinds of Changes Occur in Ecosystems?

Lesson Concept

Ecosystems change due to natural and human-made causes.

Vocabulary

succession (B52)

1. What are big changes that occur over time in ecosystems called? What can cause these big changes? _____

_____

2. Name three types of rapid changes that occur naturally in ecosystems.

_____

_____

_____

3. Describe one type of rapid change that people cause in ecosystems.

_____

_____

4. List ways that people protect themselves during rapid changes in ecosystems.

_____

_____

_____

_____

_____

Name _____

Date _____

Cleaning Up Pond Pollution

Materials

6 cups and 3 lids

wax pencil

water

pollutants

pollutants:
- food coloring, 10 drops;
- bits of paper;
- vegetable oil, 10 drops;
- carpet fibers;
- green dishwashing detergent, 10 drops;
- small pieces of bread

3 coffee filters   **3 rubber bands**   **safety goggles**   **plastic gloves**

Activity Procedure

1 Label one cup *Pollutant 1*, a second cup *Pollutant 2*, and a third *Pollutant 3*.

2 Label one of the other three cups *Filtered pollutant 1*, the second *Filtered pollutant 2*, and the third *Filtered pollutant 3*. You should now have three pairs of cups.

3 Fill each of the three pollutant cups half-full of water. **CAUTION** **Put on the safety goggles and plastic gloves.** Put two different pollutants in each cup. Put the lids on tightly, and shake each cup well.

4 **Observe** one of the cups that contain polluted water. **Record** what you see.

My observations: _____

_____

5 Push a clean coffee filter halfway into the *Filtered pollutant 1* cup. Put a rubber band around the top of the cup to hold the filter in place. Pour about half of the *Pollutant 1* water into the filter.

6 When the water has drained, **compare** the filtered water with the polluted water. **Record** your observations.

My observations: _____

_____

7 Repeat Steps 4–6 for the other two cups of polluted water.

My observations: _____

_____

Draw Conclusions

1. How were the mixtures you filtered alike? _____

_____

2. Which pollutants were filtered out? _____

_____

3. Scientists at Work Scientists **compare** samples to find the smallest differences. How did the polluted water containing oil look compared to the filtered water?

_____

_____

How did the filtered detergent mixture compare to the mixture before it was filtered? _____

_____

_____

Investigate Further Sand is sometimes used as a filter to clean water for drinking. **Form a hypothesis** about how well sand filters polluted water. **Plan and conduct an experiment** to test your hypothesis. For example, you might use the water from the activity or make "polluted" water with baby powder, flour, or other safe household materials.

_____

_____

_____

_____

Name _____

Date _____

Compare

Comparing involves noting differences between two situations or two objects.

Think About Comparing

Compare the pictures of the backyard drawn ten years apart. Circle the things in the second picture of the backyard that are different from the first picture.

May, 1990

May, 2000

Pick three of the changes in this backyard. Tell how each change may help living things that live in or near the backyard.

Change 1: _____

How it helps living things: _____

_____

Change 2: _____

How it helps living things: _____

_____

_____

Change 3: _____

How it helps living things: _____

_____

                                          Use with page B59.

Reading Skills Practice

Identify Cause and Effect

Read the selection. Find the sentences in the selection that show a cause-and-effect relationship. Write the causes and effects in the appropriate boxes below.

Reclaiming Coastal Areas

Coastal areas often require reclamation. Excessive levels of salt in the water can kill fish and other aquatic animals. Salt also can damage or kill vegetation that is planted in these areas. Ditches are constructed to drain the shallow water and, in this way, reclaim some of these marshlands. Fresh water is applied to the surface to wash out the excess salt, carry it away, and replace the drained water.

Causes:	Effects:

How Do People Change Ecosystems?

Lesson Concept

People can cause both harmful and beneficial changes to ecosystems.

Vocabulary

reclamation (B63)

Fill in the chart to describe how people affect ecosystems and how they can repair or help ecosystems.

What People Do	Effects on Ecosystem	Ways to Help Ecosystem
Spray chemicals on farmland.	1.	2.
Build dams on rivers.	3.	4.
Collect coral from reefs.	5.	6.
Cut down all trees in rain forest.	7.	8.

Answer the question below.

9. What reclamation is done today to repair damage caused by strip mining?

_____

_____

_____

Investigate Log

Using Our National Parks

Materials

7 index cards

yarn

tape recorder or video camera (optional)

Activity Procedure

1 Work with six other students. Each member of your group should role-play one of the following people:

Ten-year-old park visitor	Scientist who studies park plants
Adult park visitor	Local member of Congress
Park ranger	Reporter
Souvenir-shop owner	

2 Use the index cards and yarn to make a name tag for each group member. Use the names on the list in Step 1.

3 Below are some questions about protecting national parks. Think about how the person you are role-playing views each question. Discuss the questions with your group. Work to agree on ways to help national parks.

• Should we limit the number of people who can visit a park at any one time?

• Should we make people park their cars outside the parks and have them use buses or trains instead?

• Should we reduce the number of restaurants, snack bars, shops, and gas stations in the parks?

• Should we limit activities that harm living things in the parks, such as hiking off marked trails?

• Should we spend more money to study how to preserve national parks?

• Should we provide money to educate people about the value of national parks and about ways to keep parks healthy?

4 Use a tape recorder or a video camera to record the discussion. Review the tape to make detailed notes.

Draw Conclusions

1. Based on your discussion, **record** one or more ways to protect our national parks. Everyone in the group should agree to each way. Give reasons to support each idea. _____

   _____

   _____

   _____

2. To make your final decision, did anyone have to give up something that he or she wanted? If so, what? _____

   _____

3. **Scientists at Work** Scientists **communicate** with one another to find out new ideas. Were you respectful of one another's ideas and opinions? Did too many people try to talk at once? How could your group communicate better?

   _____

   _____

   _____

Investigate Further Make a list of the solutions your group agreed to. Find out if any of the national parks have made or plan to make these changes.

   _____

   _____

   _____

   _____

   _____

   _____

   _____

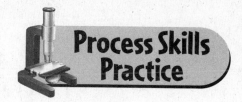

Communicate

Communicating involves both giving and receiving information.

Think About Communicating

A mining company discovered a deposit of coal beneath productive farmland. The town near this farmland is growing fast and many people are moving there. The landowner, a representative of the mining company, and two town residents are discussing what they think should be done with the land.

> I'm the landowner. This is excellent farmland that produces a lot of food for this area.
> —Landowner

> I'm from the mining company, and I want to buy this land. The grain on this land is only worth $500 per acre, but the coal is worth $200,000 per acre. We would mine this land and put a park in its place.
> —Mining Company Representative

> I'm a local resident. I think it's a bad idea. The amount of good farmland is decreasing in this country. This land could never be farmed again, and we will miss it in the future if Earth's population doesn't stop growing.
> —Local Resident

> I'm another local resident. I think the landowner would be a fool not to take your offer. This town is growing, and the people moving in need jobs. And we could really use another park.
> —Local Resident #2

1. An argument is a statement someone makes to convince others to choose an option. Which of these four people is not making an argument? Explain.

   _____

   _____

2. What might be wrong with the argument from the local resident who is in favor of selling the land? _____

   _____

   _____

3. Do you think the landowner should sell the land? Why or why not?

   _____

   _____

Use Context Clues to Determine/Confirm Word Meaning

Read the selection. Write in each box the words that give hints about the meaning of the term in bold print. Write your definition for the term on the lines provided.

Mexico Conserves Its Desert Springs

Recently conservation groups and the government of Mexico began working to conserve a large **desert springs area**. It is a 7,000-acre property in the state of Coahuila. It has a desert climate, that is, it gets very little rainfall. However, it has a lot of ponds, lakes, and streams. It also has much water in the ground. The desert springs area has aquatic animals that live in water and many types of plant life. In fact, this area is thought to be the most diverse desert springs area in the world. The property will be protected by a **conservation easement**. This is a legal agreement between a landowner and a conservation group. The landowner donates the land to the conservation group with the understanding that the conservation group will protect the land and never sell it. The agreement is in effect forever.

Term:
desert spring

Hint:

Definition:

_____

_____

Term:
conservation easement

Hint:

Definition:

_____

Name _____

Date _____

What Is Conservation?

Lesson Concept

We need to conserve our resources to protect ecosystems and meet our needs in the future.

Vocabulary

conservation (B68)   **redesign** (B71)   **preservation** (B72)

Write the letter of the best answer on the lines.

1. What do ecosystems provide for us? _____
   A wood for furniture and paper   **C** water for drinking and bathing
   B land for homes and growing food   **D** all of them

2. The careful management and wise use of natural resources is called _____.
   A reclamation   **B** conservation   **C** preservation   **D** communication

3. Three ways of reducing trash are to recycle materials, _____.
   A pick up litter off the street, and reuse things
   B buy products that have less packaging, and pick up litter off the street
   C reuse things, and buy products that have less packaging

4. What does recycling involve? _____
   A lining trash cans with old shopping bags
   B processing unused materials
   C processing used materials

5. _____ is changing a product or its packaging in order to use fewer resources.
   A Recycling   **B** Redesign   **C** Reuse   **D** Reclamation

6. One thing people CANNOT do when they set aside an area as a national park is _____.
   A redesign the land that has been set aside
   B limit where people go and how people use the park
   C help protect unusual landscapes

Name _____

Date _____

Recognize Vocabulary

Write the definition of each of the vocabulary terms, and give
three examples of each.

1. conservation

Definition: _____

Examples: _____

_____

2. preservation

Definition: _____

Examples: _____

_____

3. reclamation

Definition: _____

Examples: _____

_____

_____

4. succession

Definition: _____

Examples: _____

_____

Name _____

Date _____

Persuasive Writing

Imagine that you have been asked to write a special guest editorial for a science magazine. Write about the importance of conserving tropical rain forests. Be sure to include supporting details to convince readers of your position. Use the outline below to help you plan your editorial.

Promote Conservation

State your opinion.
State reasons. **Reason 1:**
Reason 2:
Reason 3:
Restate your opinion or call for action.

Chapter 1 • Graphic Organizer for Chapter Concepts

Earthquakes and Volcanoes

LESSON 1
EARTH'S LAYERS

Three Main Layers

1. _____

2. _____

3. _____

a. _____

b. _____

Layers that Form Plates
that Move

1. _____

2. _____

LESSON 2
EARTHQUAKES

Definition _____

Cause _____

Where Movement Occurs

_____

Point on Surface Directly Above
Where Movement Occurs

_____

How measured _____

Measuring Scales

_____

_____

LESSON 3
VOLCANOES

Definition _____

Parts of a Volcano

1. _____

2. _____

3. _____

Types of Volcanoes

1. _____

2. _____

3. _____

How Volcanoes Change the Land

1. _____

2. _____

Name _____

Date _____

The Layers of the Earth

Materials

metric ruler

half of an apple

Activity Procedure

1 **Observe** the apple half carefully. Draw a picture of this piece of the apple. Show its layers.

2 A thin peel covers the outside of the apple. Use the ruler to **measure** the thickness of the peel. **Record** your measurement on your drawing below.

3 The thick, white part that you eat is the middle of the apple. **Measure** the thickness of this layer. **Record** your measurement on your drawing below.

4 Deep inside the apple is the core. **Measure** the core, starting at the center of the apple. **Record** your measurement on your drawing below.

5 Like the apple, Earth has three layers. The crust is Earth's outside layer. The mantle is the thick, middle layer of Earth. Deep inside Earth is the core. Work with a partner to explain which parts of the apple are like the core, mantle, and crust of Earth.

Name _____

Investigate Log

Draw Conclusions

1. **Use numbers** to **compare** the layers of the apple. Which layer is the thinnest?

_____

2. Which of Earth's layers is most like the apple peel? Explain your answer.

_____

3. **Scientists at Work** Scientists use many kinds of tools to **measure** objects and their characteristics. How did using a ruler help you describe the apple's layers?

_____

_____

Investigate Further Use a small gum ball, modeling clay, and colored plastic wrap to make a cut-away model of Earth's layers. Which material will you use to stand

for the core? _____

Which material should you use to stand for the crust? _____

_____

For the mantle? _____

Tell how you could **use numbers** to make your model more accurate.

_____

_____

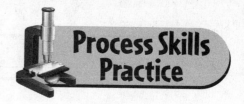

Process Skills Practice

Measure

When you use a ruler to find the height of something, you are measuring. Measuring allows you to use numbers to compare different objects in a precise manner.

Think About Measuring

Clark's teacher asks him to compare the heights of four mountains and the depths of two valleys. He is given a picture of several mountains and valleys side by side. He is told that 1 millimeter represents 200 meters of height on Earth's surface. The landforms in the picture are drawn to scale. Clark uses a metric ruler to measure the height and depth of each landform and fills in the table with his measurements.

Fill in the rest of the table with the approximate heights and depths in meters.

Landform	Measurement on Drawing in Millimeters	Approximate Distance in Meters
Mount Everest	45 high	
Anna Purna	40 high	
Aconcagua	35 high	
Mount McKinley	30 high	
Puerto Rico Trough	45 deep	
Marianas Trench	55 deep	

1. To find how much Earth's surface can vary in height and depth, Clark added the height of the tallest mountain to the depth of the deepest valley.

   What did Clark find out? _____

2. If Clark didn't use numbers, what trouble would he have when describing the

   differences between the heights of these mountains? _____

   _____

   _____

Compare and Contrast

Read the selection. Then use some signal words to write a paragraph that compares and contrasts the ways in which mountains are formed.

Mountains: The Same But Different

Mountains form in many ways. Some mountains, such as the Appalachian Mountains, rose following collisions between plates of Earth's crust. Many mountains formed where these plates collided and one plate was uplifted over another. Similar uplifting has occurred with rock movement along faults and at Earth's surface.

The Ozark Mountains in Arkansas and Missouri formed by the erosion of surface rock. Other mountains formed when plates were pulled apart and left large gaps between them. This type of movement usually occurs on the ocean floor. As magma builds up between the plates, mountains form under the ocean.

_____

_____

_____

_____

_____

_____

_____

_____

_____

_____

_____

Concept Review

What Are the Layers of the Earth?

Lesson Concept

Earth is made up of three layers: the crust, the mantle, and the core.

Vocabulary

crust (C6)	**mantle** (C6)	**core** (C6)	**plate** (C8)

Label the diagram of Earth's layers, and give a brief description of each layer.

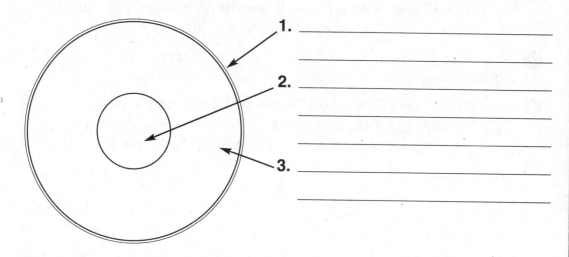

1. _____

_____

2. _____

_____

_____

3. _____

_____

Describe how the plates are moving in each diagram. Then tell where this kind of movement usually occurs and what the results are.

   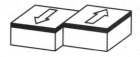

4. _____   5. _____   6. _____

_____   _____   _____

_____   _____   _____

_____   _____   _____

_____   _____   _____

_____   _____   _____

Name _____

Date _____

Earthquakes

Materials

3-in. × 5-in. self-stick note   small plastic cup   water

Activity Procedure

1 Stick the self-stick note to a table. Be sure that about 1 in. of the short side of the self-stick note is hanging over the edge of the table. Also make sure the self-stick note is firmly stuck in place.

2 Fill the cup $\frac{1}{4}$ full with water. Place the cup on the center part of the self-stick note that is on the table.

3 Carefully and firmly try to pull the self-stick note straight out from under the cup. The sticky part of the note will stop you from easily pulling it all the way out. **Observe** what happens to the water.

My observations: _____

_____

_____

_____

_____

Name _____

Draw Conclusions

1. How is snapping your fingers like the movement of the self-stick note?

_____

_____

_____

_____

_____

2. What did you **observe** about the water in the cup when you pulled on the self-stick note? _____

_____

3. Scientists at Work Scientists often **infer** things based on their observations. What can you infer might happen when plates are moving past one another if the pressure between the plates is suddenly changed? _____

_____

Investigate Further Use two 3-in. × 5-in. self-stick notes to model two plates sticking. Bend the notes so that the sticky parts face each other. Touch the sticky parts together and slide one note past the other. How does the shape of the note papers change? How do they move? _____

_____

_____

Name _____

Date _____

Observe and Infer

Observing involves using your senses to notice things around you. Inferring involves using what you observe to form an opinion. For example, you can observe a glass falling and infer that it will break when it hits the ground.

Think About Observing and Inferring

Rita learns that ocean waves caused by underwater earthquakes are called tsunamis (tsoo•NAH•meez). Tsunamis may pass through deep water unnoticed. But when tsunamis reach shallow waters near a coast, waves crest as powerful walls of water that can cause great destruction and kill people.

Rita made a table to see if earthquake strength is related to tsunami formation. She listed several famous earthquakes that occurred near large bodies of water. She recorded their strengths based on the Richter scale. On the Richter scale, higher measurements mean stronger earthquakes. Then she recorded whether or not a tsunami formed.

Location and Year of Earthquake	Measurement on the Richter Scale	Tsunami Generated
New Madrid, Missouri, 1811	approximately 7.5	yes, on the Mississippi River
Owens Valley, California, 1872	approximately 8.3	yes, in Pacific Ocean
Tokyo, Japan, 1923	approximately 8.3	yes, in Pacific Ocean
Prince William Sound, Alaska, 1964	8.6	yes, in Pacific Ocean
Southern California, 1981	4.8	no
Long Island, New York, 1981	3.7	no

1. List two observations Rita could make about tsunamis. _____

_____

_____

2. What inference could Rita make based on the data from the table?

_____

_____

Identify Cause and Effect

Read the selection. Then find three sentences in the selection—one from each paragraph—that show cause and effect. Write the sentences on the lines below. Then underline the cause and place parentheses around the effect.

The Power of Tsunamis

Earthquakes can occur suddenly, making land roll like an ocean wave. They can damage land and buildings. Often their results are deadly. But sometimes an earthquake's effects begin far from land, deep in the ocean.

Strong underwater earthquakes can make giant ocean waves called tsunamis. *Tsunami* (tsoo•nahm•ee) is Japanese for "harbor wave." Tsunamis can move in all directions from the epicenter of an earthquake. Their speeds can be up to 800 kilometers per hour. When these waves reach shore, their speeds slow to 48–80 kilometers per hour, but the waves can rise as high as 9 meters.

Like earthquakes, tsunamis can destroy. In 1703 more than 100,000 people were killed by a tsunami in Japan. More recently, a tsunami that struck Papua New Guinea in 1998 resulted in waves 7.5 meters high that killed at least 1,200 people.

_____

_____

_____

_____

_____

_____

_____

Concept Review

What Causes Earthquakes?

Lesson Concept

An earthquake is vibrations produced when energy builds up and is quickly released along a fault.

Vocabulary

earthquake (C14)	**fault** (C14)	**focus** (C15)
epicenter (C15)	**seismograph** (C16)	

Use the correct word from the list below to fill in the blanks.

brick	faults	Mercalli	plates	earthquake
epicenter	focus	Richter	seismograph	

Earth's crust is broken into _____ that move relative to one another. Breaks between plates are known as _____. Plates slide past each other along these breaks. However, sometimes rocks from two different plates stick together along a fault. Great pressure can build up in these rocks, and become so great that the rocks suddenly break apart. This releases waves of energy and causes the plates to move with a sudden jolt. We call this shaking in Earth's crust a(n) _____.

Earthquakes usually center around a single point under Earth's surface, called the _____. The point on Earth's surface right above this spot is the

_____.

Earthquakes are measured with an instrument called a _____. Scientists use information from this instrument to measure the energy an earthquake releases. They use this information to rate the earthquake on a scale, called the _____ scale. This scale generally uses the numbers from 1 to 9, with a thirtyfold increase in energy from one number to the next. Major earthquakes register at 6 or higher.

Another way to measure earthquakes is by looking at the damage they cause, using the _____ scale. This scale uses Roman numerals from I to XII. An earthquake that measures III on this scale causes a hanging lamp to swing.

An earthquake that measures X causes _____ buildings to crumble.

Volcanic Eruptions

Materials

1-L plastic bottle

funnel

air pump

puffed rice cereal or tiny pieces of plastic foam

small piece of modeling clay

aluminum pie plate

Activity Procedure

1 Ask your teacher to make a hole near the bottom of the bottle. Use the clay to stick the bottom of the bottle to the pie plate.

2 Use the funnel to fill the bottle $\frac{1}{4}$ full with the rice cereal or foam.

3 Attach the air pump to the hole in the bottle. Put a piece of clay around the hole to seal it.

4 Pump air into the bottle. **Observe** what happens.

My observations: _____

_____

_____

_____

_____

Name _____

Draw Conclusions

1. What happened to the cereal when you pumped air into the bottle?

   _____

2. How could you make more cereal shoot out of the bottle?

   _____

3. **Scientists at Work** Scientists often **make a model** to help them understand things that happen in nature. How is the bottle used to model an erupting

   volcano? _____

   _____

   _____

Investigate Further Some volcanoes have steep sides. Others have gently sloping sides. Make models using some fine sand and gravel to test this **hypothesis**: a volcano is steeper if it forms from thicker lava. What property of lava is modeled by the size of the pieces of sand and gravel? What are some other materials you

could use to model lava? _____

_____

_____

_____

_____

Name _____

Date _____

Make a Model

Making a model can help you visualize and understand something you might have a hard time observing.

Think About Making a Model

Thomas wanted to understand what happens when two plates move away from each other at the bottom of the Atlantic Ocean. He decided to make a model using two sponges and three different colors of modeling clay. The sponges represented the two plates. The modeling clay represented molten rock (lava) coming up through a fault and forming new crust. The pictures show how Thomas's model worked. Each of the different colors of clay represents molten rock of different ages.

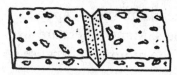

Stage 1

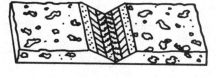

Stage 3

Stage 2

1. Thomas made a color key like the one at the right to show the ages of the molten rock in his model. Show how you think Thomas filled in his key. (If crayons or markers are not available, write the name of the color near the box.) Color or label the layers in the model to match the key.

Key

☐ oldest rock

☐ middle-aged rock

☐ youngest rock

2. Thomas later read that scientists have mapped the ocean floor in areas where two plates are pulling apart. They have found that on both sides of the fault, the oldest rocks are farthest from the fault and the youngest rocks are closest to the fault. The rocks also form a striped pattern in terms of their magnetic properties. Based on this information, do you think Thomas's model is an accurate one? Why or why not? _____

_____

_____

_____

Use Reference Sources

Read the selection. Then determine which of the following entries would be most helpful to you in finding out more information about Mount Fuji's snow-capped peak: Japan's national parks, Japanese art, volcanoes, Mount Fuji, or Japanese culture. Then use an encyclopedia to locate additional facts about the mountain's cone.

Meet Mount Fuji

In Japan and throughout the world, Mount Fuji is one of the best-known dormant volcanoes. Fuji is Japan's highest mountain. The mountain is part of Fuji-Hakone-Izu National Park. This park is the most popular vacation area in Japan.

Mount Fuji has been dormant for nearly 300 years. Its last eruption was in 1707. The eruption lasted almost two months. Because of its beautiful snow-capped peak, Mount Fuji inspires artists, photographers, and poets. Many others are also inspired by Mount Fuji. Each year, religious groups visit the mountain because they believe it to be a sacred place.

_____

_____

_____

_____

_____

_____

_____

_____

_____

_____

_____

_____

_____

_____

Use with page C23.

Name _____

Date _____

How Do Volcanoes Form?

Lesson Concept

A volcano is a crack in Earth's crust through which lava flows out onto Earth's surface.

Vocabulary

volcano (C20)	**magma** (C20)	**lava** (C20)
vent (C20)	**magma chamber** (C21)	**crater** (C22)

Answer the questions below about volcanoes.

1. Describe three ways volcanoes form. _____

_____

_____

_____

_____

_____

2. Name three different kinds of volcanic mountains, and describe how each

   forms. _____

_____

_____

_____

_____

_____

3. List three ways that volcanoes can be harmful. Tell how volcanic eruptions can

   also be helpful. _____

_____

_____

_____

Recognize Vocabulary

Write the letter of the best answer on the lines.

focus	**lava**	**fault**	**vent**
plate	**crust**	**magma**	**crater**
mantle	**epicenter**	**core**	

1. Earth's outermost layer is the _____.
   A core   **B** crust   **C** mantle   **D** plate

2. The middle of Earth's three layers is the _____.
   A core   **B** crust   **C** mantle   **D** plate

3. The innermost layer of Earth is the _____.
   A core   **B** crust   **C** mantle   **D** plate

4. A volcano can fall in on itself, creating a large basin called _____.
   A a crater   **B** an epicenter   **C** a fault   **D** a plate

5. A break in Earth's crust along which rocks move is called _____.
   A an earthquake   **B** an epicenter   **C** a fault   **D** a volcano

6. The point underground where earthquake's movement first takes place is
   called the _____.
   A crater   **B** epicenter   **C** fault   **D** focus

7. The point on Earth's surface right above the spot where the first movement
   of an earthquake occurs is called the earthquake's _____.
   A crater   **B** epicenter   **C** fault   **D** focus

8. Melted rock that reaches Earth's surface is called _____.
   A crust   **B** iron   **C** lava   **D** magma

9. Melted rock inside Earth is called _____.
   A crust   **B** iron   **C** lava   **D** magma

10. A _____ is the tube in a volcano that carries hot melted rock to the surface.
   A crater   **B** fault   **C** magma chamber   **D** vent

Use with pages C4–C25.

Writing Practice

Write a Story About Earth's Layers

Narrative Writing—Story

Imagine that you are able to travel in a protected glass elevator from the surface of Earth to the planet's core. Write a story about what you see as you travel. Use colorful, descriptive language to describe Earth's layers as accurately as you can. Use the story map below to help you plan your writing.

Describe the setting (glass elevator):
What do you see as you descend?
What do you see when the elevator reaches the planet's core?
What was your favorite part of the journey?

Fossils

LESSON 1
FOSSIL FORMATION

How Fossils Form

1. _____

_____

2. _____

_____

Types of Trace Fossils

1. _____ 2. _____

3. _____ 4. _____

5. _____

Other Fossil Types

1. _____ 2. _____

3. _____ 4. _____

5. _____

LESSON 2
WHAT FOSSILS TELL US

How Living Things Have Changed

1. _____

2. _____

3. _____

Importance of Fossils

1. _____

2. _____

3. _____

LESSON 3
HOW FOSSIL FUELS FORM

How Fossils Fuels Form

1. _____ 2. _____

3. _____

Stage 1. _____

Stage 2. _____

Stage 3. _____

Type of Coal

1. _____ 2. _____

3. _____ 4. _____

Making a Fossil

Materials

8 sugar cubes

strainer

warm water

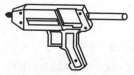
glue gun, low temperature

sink or large bowl

CAUTION ## Activity Procedure

1 Glue together four sugar cubes to make one 2 × 2 layer. **CAUTION** **The tip of the glue gun is hot.** Make a second 2 × 2 layer with the other four cubes. Let the layers dry for five minutes.

2 Spread glue on top of one layer, and place the second layer on top of it. Let the glue dry overnight.

3 Put the two-layered structure in the strainer. Put the strainer in the sink or over a bowl. Pour warm water over the structure and **observe** what happens.

My Observations: _____

_____

_____

_____

4 What happens to the sugar? _____

Does anything happen to the dried glue? _____

_____

Name _____

Draw Conclusions

1. In your model what parts of a plant or an animal did the sugar cubes

   stand for? _____

   What parts of a plant or an animal did the dried glue stand for?

   _____

   _____

2. In your model, what process did the warm water stand for? _____

   _____

   _____

3. **Scientists at Work** Scientists often **make inferences** based on their
   observations. What can you infer about how fossils form, based on

   what you learned in the investigation? _____

   _____

   _____

Investigate Further Do you think fossils are still being made? **Form a hypothesis**
about how the soft and hard parts of a piece of cooked chicken will change if it is
buried and left alone for a couple of weeks. **Plan and conduct an experiment** to
test your hypothesis. Be sure to wear goggles and rubber gloves when you handle
the meat after it has been buried. What else do you think must happen for a piece
of chicken to become a fossil?

_____

_____

_____

_____

_____

_____

Name _____

Date _____

Infer

When you infer, you use knowledge or information you already have to explain something you can observe. You can infer that if you glue two sheets of paper together, they will stick together. You know this because you know glue is sticky.

Think About Inferring

When organisms die, they usually decay quickly and disappear without leaving a trace. Sometimes, however, all or part of an organism gets preserved in rock. The preserved remains of organisms are called fossils.

1. What kind of rock do you infer would be most likely to contain fossils?

   A igneous rock **B** metamorphic rock **C** sedimentary rock

2. What knowledge and observations did you use to make your inference?

   _____

   _____

   _____

3. In which of the following places would you infer fossil-bearing rocks are most likely to form?

   A in a forest **B** in a volcano **C** under a glacier **D** under the ocean

4. What knowledge and observations did you use to make your inference?

   _____

   _____

   _____

5. If you were going on a trip to collect fossils, which tools do you think would be most useful to bring along?

   A a hand lens **B** a hammer **C** a microscope **D** a computer

6. What knowledge and observations did you use to make your inference?

   _____

   _____

   _____

Name _____

Date _____

Draw Logical Conclusions

Read the selection. Then draw some logical conclusions about the topics below.

Dinosaur Fossils

Dinosaurs last roamed the earth about 66 million years ago, millions of years before human beings first appeared. Since dinosaurs were gone before humans arrived, how do we know that these large reptiles existed? In the last 200 years or so, thousands of dinosaur fossils have been discovered that provide clues to scientists about the dinosaurs that once walked our planet.

For example, scientists have learned that dinosaurs were hatched from eggs and weighed from less than 100 pounds to more than 1,100 pounds. Judging by the abundance of fossils, dinosaurs were the dominant form of land life for some 150 million years. Most dinosaurs traveled by foot. Most dinosaurs had four legs, but some moved using only their much longer hind legs. Other dinosaurs could walk using either two or four legs.

- *weight of dinosaurs* _____
  _____
  _____

- *mobility of dinosaurs* _____
  _____
  _____

How Do Fossils Form?

Lesson Concept

Fossils are the remains of living things that lived on Earth long ago.

Vocabulary

fossil (C36)	**trace fossil** (C37)	**mold** (C38)	**cast** (C38)

Answer the questions below about fossils.

1. A crab shell is buried in sediments. The sediments get pressed and squeezed into stone. Meanwhile, the crab shell gets washed away, leaving a hollow space the shape of the crab shell. What kind of fossil is this? _____

2. An insect is trapped in the sap of an evergreen tree. The tree sap hardens to form a clear, yellow material. The entire body of the insect is preserved. What is the material that holds the fossil called? _____

3. A leaf is buried in sediments. The sediments are exposed to high heat and pressure. As this happens, most of the chemicals in the leaf evaporate. The only thing that remains is a thin, black film that is in the shape of the leaf. What is this kind of fossil called? _____

4. A tree trunk is buried in sediments. Minerals slowly take the place of the materials that formed the tree trunk. Even the structures of the cells are preserved. What do we call a fossil that forms in this way?

_____

5. Fossil footprints of an extinct kind of elephant are preserved in rock. Tracks a snake made in sand are preserved in another kind of rock. What do we call these kinds of fossils? _____

6. A hollow space was left where a bone belonging to an ancient bird had been buried. Minerals filled in the hollow space. What do we call a fossil that forms this way? _____

Name _____

Date _____

Sets of Animal Tracks

Materials

poster board

animal footprint stamps

ink pad

markers, crayons, and colored pencils

Activity Procedure

1 On the poster board, draw a picture of an area where animal tracks are found. The picture might show a riverbank or a sandy beach.

2 Each person in your group should choose a different animal. Mark these animals' tracks on the poster board. Use the ink pad and stamps, or any of the other items. Make sure that some sets of tracks go over other sets. Keep a record of which animal made tracks first, second, third, and so on.

3 When your group has finished making tracks, trade poster boards with another group. Try to figure out the order in which the other group's tracks were made. **Record** your conclusions in an ordered list. Give reasons for the order you chose. **Compare** your conclusions with the written record of the other group's track order.

My conclusions: _____

_____

_____

Draw Conclusions

1. Did all the animals move in the same way? If not, how could you tell the kind of animal from the tracks it made? _____

_____

_____

_____

2. How did your group decide which tracks were made first?

_____

_____

_____

_____

3. Scientists at Work Scientists can **infer** relationships among rock layers and the fossils they contain. They do this after carefully **observing** the rocks and fossils. What observations led you to infer the order in which the footprints were

made? _____

_____

Investigate Further Get a potato. Using a plastic knife, carefully carve the potato into an animal track stamp. Use an ink pad and the stamp to make some tracks on a sheet of paper. Have a classmate **infer** from the tracks how the "animal" moves. Does it slither? Does it walk on two legs or four legs? Or does the animal

jump or fly to get from place to place? _____

_____

_____

_____

_____

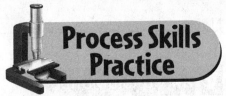

Observe and Infer

Observing involves examining objects carefully. Inferring involves using those observations to come up with an explanation about something related to the objects.

Think About Observing and Inferring

Tamara learns that scientists have found many fossil skeletons of ocean-dwelling reptiles called plesiosaurs (PLEE•see•uh•sahrz). These animals have bones similar to those of other reptiles. Scientists are not sure what the plesiosaurs preyed on. They found a fossil plesiosaur with the remains of many fossil shellfish in the place where the plesiosaur's stomach may have been. The plesiosaur might have eaten these shellfish.

Tamara observes a picture of a plesiosaur. She sees that it has flippers and swims in the oceans. She notes that its jawbone is long and narrow. The jawbone has many long, sharp teeth.

1. On the chart below, list the observations and inferences Tamara made. The inferences may be stated or implied.

Observations	Inferences

2. What are some other possible inferences Tamara could have made about the shellfish found with the plesiosaurs? _____

_____

_____

Use Context Clues to Determine/Confirm Word Meaning

Read the selection. Then complete the chart below.

The Amazing Shark

There are more than 350 varieties of sharks. Sharks vary greatly in their size, behavior, and method of reproduction. Scientists who have studied sharks have discovered that the species probably evolved from primitive fish called placoderms (PLACK•uh•dermz). Sharks have continued to evolve and adapt to their environments.

Most sharks swim constantly, but usually at a leisurely pace. However, they have the capacity to increase their speed to about 65 kilometers per hour when necessary. Perhaps the most distinctive feature of sharks, one that has helped them survive for millions of years, is their well-developed sensory system. Their eyes can see in dim light and can recognize contrasts of light and shadow easily. Their sense of smell is extremely strong, making it possible to detect prey at long distances.

Shark Adaptation	Purpose of Adaptation
ability to swim at rapid speeds	
strong eyesight	
strong hearing	

Name _____

Date _____

What Can We Learn from Fossils?

Lesson Concept

Fossils tell us about living things of the past, how living things have changed over time, and how Earth has changed.

Answer the questions below.

1. How can scientists use the order of rock layers to learn about the ages of

   different rocks? _____

2. Scientists study rock layers. What evidence do they gather from their studies?

   _____

   _____

3. Name and describe two living things that have changed over time.

   _____

   _____

   _____

   _____

4. Give an example of an animal that has changed over the span of geologic time.
   Tell how scientists know about these changes. What do these changes also tell

   about how Earth has changed over time? _____

   _____

   _____

   _____

Use with page C49.

What Kinds of Rocks Store Petroleum?

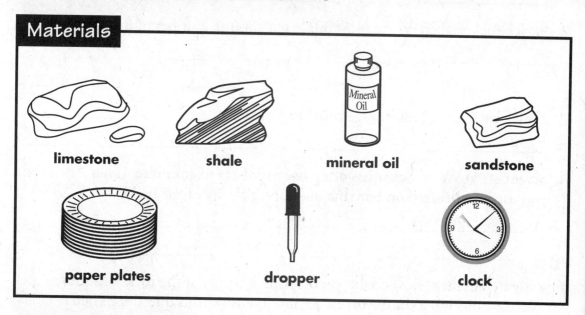

limestone   shale   mineral oil   sandstone

paper plates   dropper   clock

Activity Procedure

1. Place the rock samples on separate paper plates. **Observe** each rock. **Predict** which will be the best storage rock.

2. Fill the dropper with mineral oil. Put 5 drops of oil on the limestone sample.

3. **Observe** and **record** the time it takes for the 5 drops of oil to soak into the limestone.

4. Continue adding oil, counting the drops, until the limestone will hold no more oil. **Record** the number of drops it takes.

5. Repeat Steps 2–4 with the other rock samples.

Name _____

Investigate Log

Draw Conclusions

1. Which rock soaked up the oil the fastest? What was the time?

_____

_____

2. Which rock soaked up the most oil? What was the number of drops?

_____

_____

3. Which rock is the best storage rock? Explain. _____

_____

4. Scientists at Work Scientists often **use numbers** to **compare** things. How did you use numbers to compare the oil-storing ability of the rocks?

_____

_____

Investigate Further How could you determine which of the rocks is a source rock for petroleum? **Plan a simple investigation** to answer this question. Then decide what equipment you would need to carry out this investigation. _____

_____

_____

_____

Name _____

Date _____

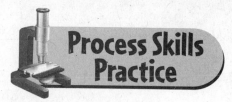

Use Numbers and Compare

Numbers give you a way to estimate things. They allow you to count, order, or compare information.

Think About Using Numbers and Comparing

The table below on the left shows how many quadrillion Btus (a way of measuring energy) were used in 1995 by the countries listed. Find the largest number in the "Btus" column. Put that number at the top of the Btus column in the table on the right. Next to that number, write the name of the country that used that amount of energy. Complete the table, ordering the numbers from largest to smallest.

Country	Btus
Germany	13.71
United Kingdom	9.85
China	35.67
Italy	7.42
Russia	26.75
Canada	11.72
United States	90.94
Japan	21.42
France	9.43
India	10.50

Btus	Country

1. What is the total energy used by the five European countries listed? What is the total energy used by the three Asian countries? How do these figures compare?

_____

_____

2. What did you learn from adding and comparing the numbers showing European and Asian energy use? _____

_____

_____

Use with page C51.

Name _____

Date _____

Compare and Contrast

Read the selection. Then complete the graphic to show how the process of making paper is similar to and different from the techniques used in ancient times.

Making Paper: Then and Now

The paper you write on has a very long history. The Egyptians made the first paper about 5,500 years ago! First, they soaked papyrus (puh•PY•ruhs), which is a tall plant that grows near water in the Middle East. When the papyrus was ready, the Egyptians cut it into fine strips, pounded it into a pulp, and shaped the pulp into thin sheets.

About 3,000 years later, the Chinese developed a papermaking process of their own. The Chinese used chemicals to turn straw, wood, and rags into pulp. Then they bleached the pulp, washed it, and rolled it into sheets.

Today, paper largely is made by machines, but the methods for making pulp are similar to those used by the Egyptians and the Chinese. Newspaper and other inexpensive types of paper are made by mechanically pulverizing wood. Then the pulp is treated with chemicals. Finer, more expensive papers are made with pulp and scrap cloth.

Similar	**Different**

Concept Review

How Do Fossil Fuels Form?

Lesson Concept

Fossil fuels form over millions of years from the decayed remains of organisms. Coal forms in four stages, first forming peat, then lignite, then bitumen, and finally anthracite.

Vocabulary

peat (C55)   **lignite** (C55)   **bituminous coal** (C55)

anthracite (C55)   **natural gas** (C53)   **fossil fuels** (C52)

petroleum (C53)

Write the letter of the definition in Column B next to the word it defines in Column A.

Column A

_____ 70 percent

_____ anthracite

_____ the sun

_____ sedimentary

_____ petroleum

_____ bitumen

_____ swamps

_____ coal

_____ seams

_____ fossil fuels

_____ natural gas

_____ lignite

_____ peat

_____ petrochemicals

Column B

A coal, natural gas, and petroleum

B the most common fossil fuel

C fossil fuel that formed when microorganisms died and fell to the bottoms of ancient seas

D first stage of coal formation

E soft, brown rock that forms as layers of sand and mud cover peat

F mostly methane, usually found with petroleum

G source of the energy in fossil fuels

H third stage of coal formation

I chemicals made from petroleum

J kind of rock in which fossil fuels are usually found

K layers of coal

L fourth stage of coal formation

M places where peat can be found

N amount of carbon in lignite

Use with page C57.

Name _____

Date _____

Recognize Vocabulary

Review the vocabulary terms for Chapter 2 by completing this word puzzle.

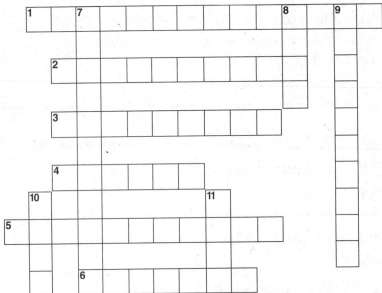

Across

1. This most useful type of fuel is used in factories and electric power stations. (2 words)

2. A fossil fuel consisting mostly of methane (2 words)

3. The world's most widely used fossil fuel

4. The remains of a once-living organism

5. The products of once-living organisms, such as coal, natural gas, and oil (2 words)

6. Sometimes called brown coal, it is a light brown rock containing more carbon than peat.

Down

7. Changes made by long-dead animals that provide scientists with clues about them

8. What is formed when minerals fill a mold fossil and harden

9. A very hard, black rock that is a valued form of coal

10. An imprint made by the outside of dead plants or animals

11. A dark yellow or brown crumbly material made of dead swamp plants

Use with pages C36–C57.

Write a Friendly Letter

Expressive Writing–Friendly Letter

Imagine that you were visiting the La Brea Tar Pits in Los Angeles when the first fossils were discovered. Write a letter to a friend describing what you observed. Explain how the fossils developed. Use the letter format below to help you plan your writing.

Heading
Your address:

Today's date:

Greeting

Dear _____,

Body of Letter

First Paragraph:

Second Paragraph:

Closing
Your friend,

_____

Chapter 1 • Graphic Organizer for Chapter Concepts

Weather Conditions

LESSON 1
EARTH'S ATMOSPHERE

Describe the Atmosphere

1. _____

2. _____

Four Layers of the Atmosphere

1. _____

2. _____

3. _____

4. _____

LESSON 2
AIR MASSES AFFECT WEATHER

Describe an Air Mass

1. _____

2. _____

3. _____

Fronts

1. form _____

2. cold front _____

3. warm front _____

LESSON 3
WEATHER PREDICTION

Weather Conditions and the Instruments Used to Measure Them

1. _____

2. _____

3. _____

4. _____

5. _____

Weather Maps

1. _____

2. _____

A Property of Air

Materials

metric ruler

piece of string about 80 cm long

scissors

2 round balloons
(same size)

straight pin

safety goggles

  Activity Procedure

1. Work with a partner. Use the scissors to carefully cut the string into three equal pieces. **CAUTION** **Be careful when using scissors.**

2. Tie one piece of the string to the middle of the ruler.

3. Blow up the balloons so they are about the same size. Seal the balloons. Then tie a piece of string around the neck of each balloon.

4. Tie a balloon to each end of the ruler. Hold the middle string up so that the ruler hangs from it. Move the strings so that the ruler is balanced. See Picture A on page D5.

5. **CAUTION** **Put on your safety goggles.** Use the straight pin to pop one of the balloons. **Observe** what happens to the ruler.

My observations: _____

_____

_____

Investigate Log

Draw Conclusions

1. Explain how this investigation shows that air takes up space.

_____

_____

2. Describe what happened when one balloon was popped. What property of air caused what you **observed**? _____

_____

_____

3. Scientists at Work Scientists often **infer** conclusions when the answer to a question is not clear or can't be **observed** directly. Your breath is invisible, but you observed how it made the balloons and the ruler behave. Even though you can't see air, what can you infer about whether or not air is matter? Explain.

_____

_____

_____

_____

Investigate Further The air around you presses on you and everything else on Earth. This property of air, called air pressure, is a result of air's weight. When more air is packed into a small space, air pressure increases. You can feel air pressure for yourself. Hold your hands around a partly filled balloon while your partner blows it up. Describe what happens. Then **infer** which property of air

helps keep the tires of a car inflated. _____

_____

_____

Observe and Infer

You make observations when you notice details. You make inferences when you use those details to come up with a possible explanation for why or how an event occurred.

Think About Observing and Inferring

Martha crumpled several pieces of paper and stuffed them into the bottom of a drinking glass. She pushed the glass straight down into a bowl of water. She held the glass down for one minute. During that minute nothing happened. The paper stayed where it was in the glass, and no bubbles rose to the surface of the water. Then Martha pulled the glass straight out of the water. She pulled the paper out of the bottom of the drinking glass. The paper and the inside of the glass were dry.

1. Fill in the table below with observations Martha made.

When Observation Was Made	Observation
Before the experiment	
During the experiment	
During the experiment	
After the experiment	

2. What inferences might Martha make from her observations? _____

_____

_____

_____

_____

Use Reference Sources

Read the selection. Then use reference sources to locate information about the elements that make up Mars' atmosphere. Use the information and percentages to complete the chart.

The Red Planet

Mars is the planet the Romans named after the god of war. It is the next planet beyond Earth's orbit as you travel out from the sun. At times it is the third-brightest object in the night sky after the moon and Venus. Unlike Venus, Mars has a thin atmosphere. Heat escapes quickly from the surface. So, the surface of Mars is much colder than the surface of Venus. Two satellites orbit Mars. Each satellite is only a few kilometers wide and has many craters.

The Martian day is 24 hours, 37 minutes, and 23 seconds long. Mars, like Earth, is tipped on its axis, creating seasonal changes much like those on Earth. The orbit of Mars lies about 1.5 times farther from the sun than does Earth's orbit. Because Mars is farther from the sun than Earth is, it takes longer for Mars to complete a revolution. One year on Mars is 687 Earth days long.

Major Elements of Mars' Atmosphere	Percentages

Name _____

Date _____

Concept Review

What Makes Up Earth's Atmosphere?

Lesson Concept

Earth is surrounded by four thin layers of air called the atmosphere.

Vocabulary

atmosphere (D6)   **air pressure** (D7)   **troposphere** (D8)   **stratosphere** (D8)

Answer the questions below.

1. Describe how the atmosphere formed and changed over time. _____

_____

_____

_____

2. What does carbon dioxide in the atmosphere do? _____

_____

Label the diagram of the atmosphere, and describe each layer. In your descriptions, tell where the air pressure is highest and where it is lowest, where the temperature is highest and lowest, and where the ozone layer is.

3. Layer: _____

   Description: _____

   _____

4. Layer: _____

   Description: _____

   _____

5. Layer: _____   **6.** Layer: _____

   Description: _____   Description: _____

   _____   _____

   _____   _____

Use with page D9.

Workbook   WB165

Wind Speed

Materials

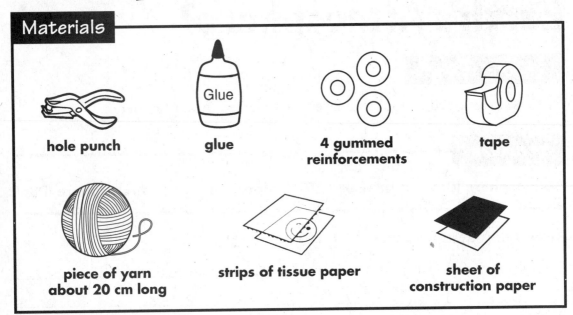

hole punch   glue   4 gummed reinforcements   tape

piece of yarn about 20 cm long   strips of tissue paper   sheet of construction paper

Activity Procedure

1. Form a cylinder with the sheet of construction paper. Tape the edge of the paper to keep the cylinder from opening.

2. Use the hole punch to make two holes at one end of the cylinder. Punch them on opposite sides of the cylinder and about 3 cm from the end. Put two gummed reinforcements on each hole, one on the inside and one on the outside.

3. Thread the yarn through the holes, and tie it tightly to form a handle loop.

4. Glue strips of tissue paper to the other end of the cylinder. Put tape over the glued strips to hold them better. Your completed windsock should look like the one shown in Picture B on page D11 of your textbook.

5. Hang your windsock outside. Use the chart on the next page to **measure** wind speed each day for several days. **Record** your measurements in a chart. Include the date, time of day, observations of objects affected by the wind, and the approximate wind speed.

Name _____

Wind Scale			
Speed in km/hr	**Description**	**Observations on Land**	**Windsock Position**
0	no breeze	no movement of wind	limp
6–19	light breeze	leaves rustle, wind vanes move, wind felt on face	slightly up
20–38	moderate breeze	dust and paper blow, small branches sway	nearly 90 degrees to arm
39–49	strong breeze	umbrellas hard to open, large branches sway	stiff and 90 degrees from arm

Draw Conclusions

1. How fast was the weakest wind you **measured**? _____

   _____

   How fast was the strongest wind? _____

2. How did you determine the speed of the wind? _____

   _____

   _____

3. **Scientists at Work** *Light, moderate,* and *strong* are adjectives describing wind speed. Scientists often **use numbers** to describe things because, in science, numbers are more exact than words. What is the wind speed measurement, in kilometers per hour, if the wind is making large tree

   branches sway? _____

Investigate Further Use a magnetic compass to determine which way is north from your windsock. **Measure** both wind speed and direction each day for a week.

Record your data in a chart.

Name _____

Date _____

Process Skills
Practice

Use Numbers

Reading measurements allows you to communicate precise information about an event.

Think About Measuring

Hurricanes are powerful storms that form near the equator over warm ocean water that is at least 27°C (81°F). In the Northern Hemisphere, hurricane winds blow in a counterclockwise direction. In the Southern Hemisphere, hurricane winds blow in a clockwise direction. To be classified as a hurricane, the winds must blow at least 119 km/hr. A hurricane swirls around an area of low air pressure. The eye of the storm is a calm region at the center of the hurricane that has the lowest air pressure and generally the highest air temperatures.

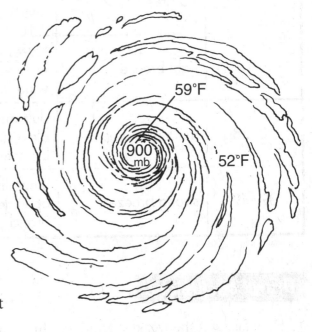

1. Normal air pressure is 985 millibars. What is the difference (in millibars) between the air pressure in the eye of the storm and normal air pressure?

   _____

2. What is the temperature difference between the eye of the storm and the main

   body of the storm? _____

3. Imagine the storm is traveling toward a coastal city 100 kilometers away at 15 km/hr. How long would it take the storm to reach the city? Show how you figured this out.

   _____

4. Which hemisphere could this storm form in? Explain your answer.

   _____
   _____

Identify Cause and Effect

Read the selection. Find the sentences in the selection that show a cause-and-effect relationship. Write the causes and effects in the appropriate boxes below.

Here Come the Monsoons

The monsoon winds have a strong effect on the climate in parts of Asia. For about six months of the year, cool, dry winds blow down from the Himalayas and dry out the ground. Beginning in May the monsoon winds reverse direction and bring warm, wet air masses from the ocean. Rain falls in torrents and widespread flooding occurs. Agriculture here depends on the monsoons and the rain they bring. If the monsoons do not come, crops fail and there is danger of famine.

Causes:

Effects:

How Do Air Masses Affect Weather?

Lesson Concept

The sun warms Earth unevenly, forming air masses of different temperatures.

Vocabulary

cirrus (D15)	**cumulus** (D15)	**cumulonimbus** (D15)	**stratus** (D15)
greenhouse effect (D12)		**air mass** (D13)	**front** (D14)

Fill in the blanks below by describing what happens to the sun's radiation.

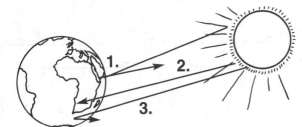

1. _____

2. _____

3. _____

Label the key for the weather map.

Key

4. _____

5. _____

6. _____

7. _____

8. Describe a warm front, and tell what happens as a warm front moves through

an area. _____

_____

_____

_____

Name _____

Date _____

Air Pressure

Materials

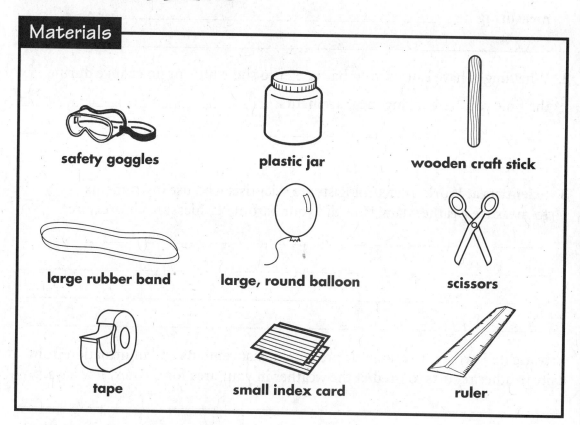

safety goggles

plastic jar

wooden craft stick

large rubber band

large, round balloon

scissors

tape

small index card

ruler

CAUTION

Activity Procedure

1 **CAUTION** **Put on your safety goggles. Be careful when using scissors.** Use the scissors to carefully cut the neck off the balloon.

2 Have your partner hold the jar while you stretch the balloon over the open end. Make sure the balloon fits snugly over the jar. Secure the balloon with the rubber band.

3 Tape the craft stick to the top of the balloon. Make sure that more than half of the craft stick stretches out from the edge of the jar.

4 On the blank side of the index card, use a pencil and a ruler to make a thin line. Label the line *Day 1*. Tape the card to a wall. Make sure the line is at the same height as the wooden stick on your barometer. See Picture B on page D19.

5 At the same time each day for a week, **measure** relative air pressure by marking the position of the wooden stick on the index card. Write the correct day next to each reading.

Investigate Log

Draw Conclusions

1. Describe how air pressure changed during the time that you were **measuring** it. _____

_____

2. What might have caused your barometer to show little or no change during the time you were taking **measurements**? _____

_____

_____

3. Scientists at Work Meteorologists are scientists who use instruments to **measure** weather data. How did your barometer measure air pressure?

_____

_____

_____

_____

Investigate Further Use your air pressure **measurements** and information from daily weather reports to **predict** the weather in your area for the next few days.

_____

_____

_____

_____

Name _____

Date _____

Measure

By measuring carefully, you can learn how weather conditions change from day to day.

Think About Measuring

Read the barometers below, and record the measurements of air pressure. Then answer the question.

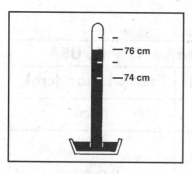

Day 1

Air Pressure
Measurement: _____

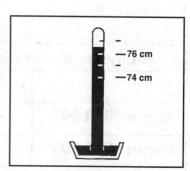

Day 2

Air Pressure
Measurement: _____

Day 3

Air Pressure
Measurement: _____

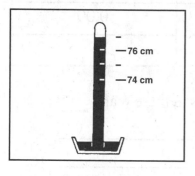

Day 4

Air Pressure
Measurement: _____

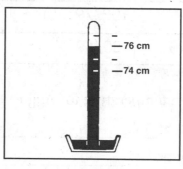

Day 5

Air Pressure
Measurement: _____

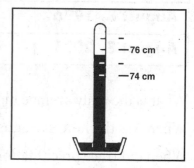

Day 6

Air Pressure
Measurement: _____

1. Air pressure at sea level is at its average when it reads 76 cm (29.5 in.) on the mercury barometer. On which days is a high pressure system moving through?

When might a front, bringing low pressure be on its way? _____

_____

_____

Name _____

Date _____

Use Graphic Sources for Information

Check It Out

Cities throughout the world keep records of high and low temperatures for each date, as well as the amount of precipitation. Use the chart below to answer the questions.

Daily Temperature Data/Precipitation Data for City Q, USA		
	Daily High/ Daily Low (°F)	**Precipitation (cm)**
August 8, 1898	83/65	trace
August 8, 1909	72/68	0.00
August 8, 1921	94/76	0.64
August 8, 1945	85/70	6.4
August 8, 1974	77/68	trace
August 8, 1996	102/79	0.00
August 8, 2001	80/59	1.9

What is the daily average high temperature for August 8 in these years? ____

When was the hottest August 8? _____

When did trace precipitation occur? _____

In which years was there no precipitation on August 8? _____

Concept Review

How Is Weather Predicted?

Lesson Concept

Meteorologists use many kinds of tools to help them predict weather.

Vocabulary

barometer (D20)   **humidity** (D21)   **hygrometer** (D21)

Read each statement, and decide whether it is true or false. On the line, write *True* if the statement is true or *False* if the statement is false.

_____ **1.** You can measure air pressure with a thermometer.

_____ **2.** Most cold air masses have higher air pressure than most warm air masses.

_____ **3.** The amount of moisture in the air is called humidity.

_____ **4.** Cool air holds more moisture than warm air does.

_____ **5.** Meteorologists measure wind speed using a barometer.

Use the weather map to answer the questions.

6. What states shown have a warm front? _____

7. What states shown have a cold front? _____

8. What states shown have rain? _____

9. If you were a meteorologist, what kind of weather would you predict Santa Fe, New Mexico will have tomorrow? Little Rock, Arkansas? _____

_____

Use with page D23.

Recognize Vocabulary

atmosphere	air pressure	troposphere
stratosphere	greenhouse effect	air mass
front	barometer	humidity
anemometer		

For each pair of terms, write how they are the same and different in meaning.

1. stratosphere and troposphere

_____

_____

_____

2. air mass and front

_____

_____

_____

3. barometer and anemometer

_____

_____

_____

Match each term in Column A with its meaning in Column B.

Column A

_____ **4.** humidity

_____ **5.** greenhouse effect

_____ **6.** atmosphere

_____ **7.** air pressure

Column B

A pressure caused by air particles pressing down on Earth's surface

B amount of water vapor in the air

C layers of air surrounding Earth

D effect of air trapping heat around Earth

Informative Writing

Explain How to Measure Weather

Write a brochure explaining how to use a thermometer and a barometer to make weather measurements. Use the outline below to help you plan your writing.

Thermometer	Barometer
What it looks like	**What it looks like**
What it measures	**What it measures**
Unit of measurement	**Unit of measurement**

How to use it
 	
  First:
 	
  Next:
 	
  Finally:
	How to use it
	
	  First:
	
	  Next:
	
	  Finally:

Chapter 2 • Graphic Organizer for Chapter Concepts

The Oceans

LESSON 1
OCEANS AND THE WATER CYCLE

1. The _____ is how water circulates through Earth's oceans, atmosphere, and streams.

The Three Parts of the Water Cycle are

2. _____

3. _____

4. _____

Ocean Water is Made of

5. _____

6. _____

LESSON 2
THE MOVEMENTS OF OCEANS

Movement Types

1. _____

2. _____

3. _____

   a. _____

   b. _____

LESSON 3
THE OCEAN FLOOR

Shore Zone

1. _____

2. _____

Abyssal Plain

1. _____

2. _____

Mid-Ocean Ridge

1. _____

2. _____

3. _____

Trench

1. _____

Getting Fresh Water from Salt Water

Materials

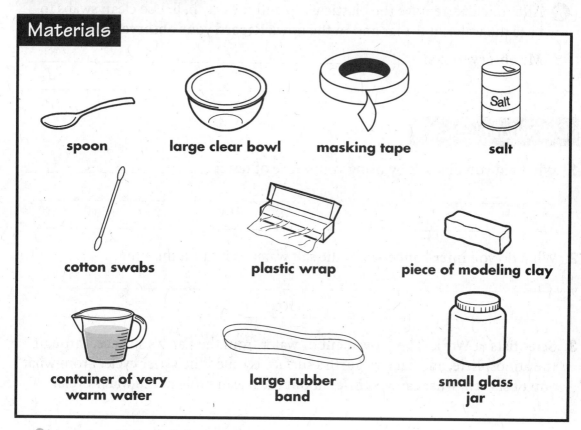

spoon

large clear bowl

masking tape

salt

cotton swabs

plastic wrap

piece of modeling clay

container of very warm water

large rubber band

small glass jar

CAUTION Activity Procedure

1 Stir two spoonfuls of salt into the container of very warm water. Put one end of a clean cotton swab into this mixture. Taste the mixture by touching the swab to your tongue. **Record** your **observations.** **CAUTION** **Don't share swabs. Don't put a swab that has touched your mouth back into any substance. Never taste anything in an investigation or experiment unless you are told to do so.**

My observations: _____

_____

2 Pour the salt water into the large bowl. Put the jar in the center of the bowl of salt water.

3 Put the plastic wrap over the top of the bowl. The wrap should not touch the top of the jar inside the bowl. Put a large rubber band around the bowl to hold the wrap in place.

④ Form the clay into a small ball. Put the ball on top of the plastic wrap right over the jar. Make sure the plastic wrap doesn't touch the jar.

⑤ On the outside of the bowl, use tape to mark the level of the salt water. Place the bowl in a sunny spot for one day.

⑥ After one day, remove the plastic wrap and the clay ball. Use clean swabs to taste the water in the jar and in the bowl. **Record** your **observations**.

My observations: _____

_____

Draw Conclusions

1. What did you **observe** by using your sense of taste? _____

_____

_____

2. What do you **infer** happened to the salt water as it sat in the sun?

_____

_____

3. Scientists at Work The movement of water from the Earth's surface, through the atmosphere, and back to Earth's surface is called the water cycle. From what you **observed,** what can you **infer** about the ocean's role in the water cycle?

_____

_____

_____

_____

Investigate Further Put the plastic wrap and the clay back on the large bowl. Leave the bowl in the sun for several days, until all the water in the large bowl is gone. **Observe** the bowl and the jar. What can you **conclude** about ocean water?

_____

_____

_____

_____

Name _____

Date _____

Observe and Infer

You use your senses to make observations. You use these observations to make inferences, which are explanations or opinions, about what you have observed.

Think About Observing and Inferring

Eugene wanted to demonstrate to his friends that different bodies of water contain different amounts of salts. He found a table that showed the amount of salt dissolved in the water from lakes and oceans in different parts of the world. He used the table to help mix samples of water with varying salinity. Then he asked his friends to taste his samples and rate them for saltiness.

Ranking (Least Salty to Most Salty)	Sample
1	E
2	A
3	D
4	F
5	B
6	C

Body of Water	Salinity	Sample
Atlantic Ocean	35 g/1000 g	
Arctic Ocean	31 g/1000 g	
Black Sea	15 g/1000 g	
Dead Sea	300 g/1000 g	
Great Salt Lake	200 g/1000 g	
Lake Superior	<1g/1000 g	

1. The table on the left gives the ranking of the samples by Eugene's friends. Which sample did they rank the saltiest? Which sample did they rank the least salty?

_____

2. The table on the right gives the salinity of different bodies of water. Based on the tables above, infer which of the samples corresponds to which body of water. Then, fill in the right column of the table.

3. Eugene told his friends that they had made an error in their ranking. He said that Sample D was actually saltier than Sample F. Do you think his friends were careless in their work? Explain your answer. _____

_____

Name _____

Date _____

Use Graphic Sources for Information

Look at the illustration below. Identify four nouns in the illustration. For each noun, write a sentence about how the thing it names contributes to the water cycle.

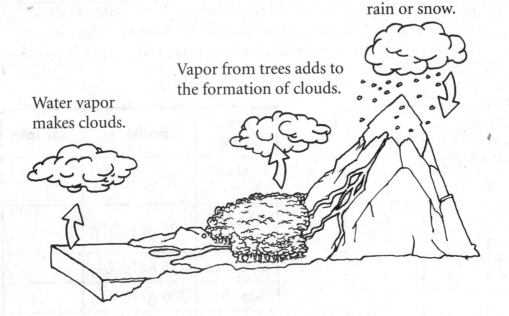

Clouds release rain or snow.

Vapor from trees adds to the formation of clouds.

Water vapor makes clouds.

1. Noun: _____

Sentence: _____

_____

2. Noun: _____

Sentence: _____

_____

3. Noun: _____

Sentence: _____

_____

4. Noun: _____

Sentence: _____

What Role Do Oceans Play in the Water Cycle?

Lesson Concept

The interactions between the oceans, other bodies of water, the sun, and the land cause the recycling of most of Earth's water.

Vocabulary

water cycle (D34)   **evaporation** (D34)

condensation (D34)   **precipitation** (D35)

Define the following terms, and show where each occurs in the diagram of the water cycle.

1. Evaporation: _____

_____

2. Condensation: _____

_____

3. Precipitation: _____

_____

_____

For each of the places listed, say whether the ocean water is saltier than average, of average saltiness, or less salty than average.

4. _____ in the middle of a large ocean

5. _____ near the North Pole

6. _____ near the equator

7. _____ where a river flows into the ocean

Name _____

Date _____

Water Currents

Materials

| clear, medium-sized bowl | colored ice cube | clock | warm tap water |

Activity Procedure

1. Put the bowl on a flat surface. Carefully fill the bowl three-quarters full of warm tap water.

2. Let the water stand undisturbed for 10 minutes.

3. Without stirring the warm water or making a splash, gently place the colored ice cube in the middle of the bowl.

4. **Observe** for 10 minutes what happens as the ice cube melts. Every 2 minutes, make a simple drawing of the bowl to **record** your observations.

   My observations: _____

   _____

   _____

   _____

   _____

Name _____

Draw Conclusions

1. Describe what you **observed** as the ice cube melted in the bowl of warm water.

_____

_____

_____

_____

2. In your **model**, what does the bowl of water stand for? _____

_____

What does the ice cube stand for? _____

3. Since the liquid in the bowl and the ice cube were both water, what can you **infer** about the cause of what happened in the bowl? _____

_____

_____

_____

4. Scientists at Work In Chapter 1, you learned that cold air is denser than warm air. The same is true for water. Using this information and what you **observed** in the investigation, explain one way ocean currents form. _____

_____

_____

_____

Investigate Further Mix up two batches of salt water. Use twice as much salt in one batch as in the other. Use the water to **model** another kind of ocean current. Fill a clear bowl three-fourths full with the less salty water. Add a few drops of food coloring to the saltier water. Along the side of the bowl, slowly pour the colored, saltier water into the clear, less salty water. Describe your **observations**. **Make a hypothesis** to explain what you observed. What **prediction** can you make based on the hypothesis? **Plan and conduct a simple investigation** to test your hypothesis. _____

_____

_____

_____

Observe

You can observe a model to see how salt water mixes with fresh water
and how the water moves in an estuary.

Think About Observing a Model

David wanted to see if salt water and fresh water mix evenly in an
estuary. He did the following experiment. He filled a bowl half-full of
fresh water. He filled another bowl one-third full of salt water. He put
red food coloring in the salt water and let the two bowls reach room
temperature. Then he slowly poured the salt water into the fresh water,
along the side of the bowl.

1. What was David trying to find out with his model? How did adding food
   coloring to the salt water aid his observations? _____

   _____

   _____

   _____

   _____

2. After David poured the salt water into the fresh water, what do you think he
   focused on observing? _____

   _____

   _____

   _____

3. David watched the bowl of water for a few minutes. He noted that the red-
   colored water sank to the bottom of the bowl and a layer of clear water floated
   on top of the colored layer. Based on David's observations of this model, do
   you think he would expect to find salt water and fresh water evenly mixed in

   an estuary? Explain your answer. _____

   _____

   _____

   _____

Use with page D39.

Compare and Contrast

Read the selection below. Then complete the Venn diagram by comparing and contrasting surface currents and deep ocean currents.

Water Currents

A current is a flowing movement of water in a larger body of water. There are two types of currents in the ocean. One type is known as a surface current. This is caused by wind blowing over the surface of the ocean and pushing the water along. The movement of Earth on its axis also affects this type of current. Deep ocean currents are the flowing of water far beneath the surface. Differences in density caused by saltiness or temperature affect the way water moves. Water that is colder or saltier sinks beneath water that is warmer or less salty, making a current.

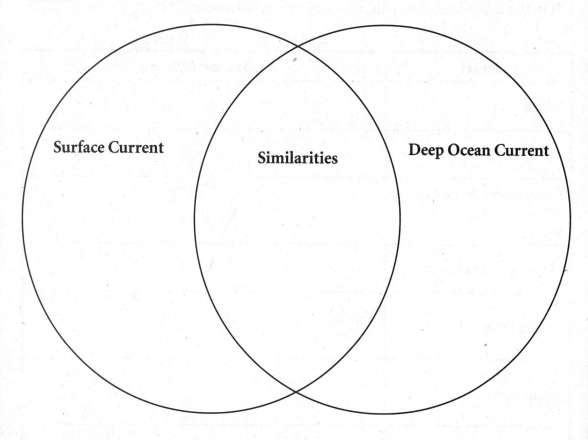

Surface Current   Similarities   Deep Ocean Current

What Are the Motions of Oceans?

Lesson Concept

The water in the ocean moves in many different ways.

Vocabulary

wave (D40)	**storm surge** (D41)	**tide** (D42)
deep ocean current (D44)	**surface current** (D44)	

Fill in the cause-and-effect chart about ocean movements.

Effect	Cause or Causes
Waves	
Storm surge	
Erosion and deposition of sediments along the shore	
Daily high and low tides	
Spring tides	
Neap tides	
Surface currents	
Deep ocean currents	

Name _____

Date _____

Model the Ocean Floor

Materials

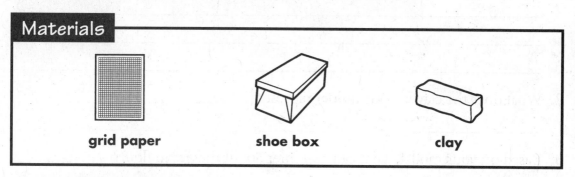

grid paper   shoe box   clay

Activity Procedure

1 Set up a graph as shown at the top of page D47. Label the horizontal axis *Distance East of New Jersey (km)*. Label the vertical axis *Water Depth (m)*.

2 Look closely at the graph. Notice that the top horizontal mark is labeled *0*. This mark represents the surface of the ocean. The numbers beneath stand for depths below sea level.

3 Plot the chart data on the graph.

Distance (km)	Depth (m)
0	0
500	3500
2000	5600
3000	4300
4000	0
4300	3050
5000	5000
5650	0

4 Connect the points on your graph. You have now made a profile of the Atlantic Ocean floor.

5 **Analyze** your graph. Determine how the ocean floor changes as you move eastward from New Jersey.

6 Use clay to **make a model** of your profile. Label the narrow end of the shoe box *Coastline*. Label the opposite end *6000 km*. Put the clay inside the box. Vary the height of the clay to model the changing depth of the ocean floor. See Picture A on page D47.

Draw Conclusions

1. Describe what you **observed** on the graph. _____
   _____
   _____
   _____

2. What does the clay in your **model** represent? _____
   _____

3. Based on your model, what can you infer about the ocean floor? _____
   _____

4. **Scientists at Work** Sound waves travel through ocean water at about 1525
   meters per second. Suppose it takes two seconds for an echo to return. The
   sound takes one second to reach the ocean floor and one second to return, so
   the distance to the ocean floor is about 1525 meters. Using the numbers from
   the chart, at what distance from New Jersey would it take a sound wave four

   seconds to return to a ship? _____

Investigate Further Use numbers to make a chart of heights to profile one
section of your classroom. Your chart should resemble the one shown in this
activity. Exchange charts with a classmate, and try to identify the exact location

shown by the map. _____
_____
_____
_____

Use Numbers

Scientists use models, charts, and graphs to determine how the ocean floor looks. Study the graph below. Then answer the questions.

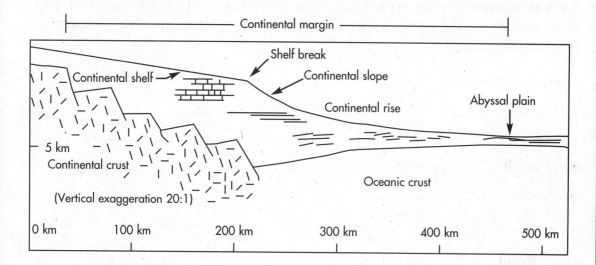

1. At what point does the continental shelf break off? _____

2. What is the difference in distance between the continental slope and the abyssal plain? _____

3. Estimate where the continental slope becomes the continental rise. _____

   _____

4. How far does the continental crust extend into the ocean? _____

Write a sentence describing the continental crust. _____

_____

Use Prefixes and Suffixes to Determine Word Meanings

Look at the words below. Write the definition of each word. Determine which part is the root word. Then write a sentence using the original word or the root word in its proper context.

abyssal

Definition: _____

_____

Root word: _____

Sentence: _____

_____

continental

Definition: _____

_____

Root word: _____

Sentence: _____

_____

undersea

Definition: _____

_____

Root word: _____

Sentence: _____

_____

What Is the Ocean Floor Like?

Lesson Concept

The features of the ocean floor are much like those on land. Ocean features include mountains, plains, trenches, valleys, and canyons. The ocean floor changes because of eruptions and shifts in Earth's plates.

Vocabulary

shore zone (D49)	**continental shelf** (D49)	**abyssal plain** (D50)
trench (D50)	**mid-ocean ridge** (D50)	

Use the vocabulary words above to fill in the blanks of the sentences below.

1. If you were standing on a large, flat area of the ocean floor, you would be at an

_____.

2. The ocean landform that is most like a valley on Earth's surface is a

_____.

3. In the middle section of the ocean is a series of mountain ranges called a

_____.

4. The part of the ocean in which you might swim is known as the

_____.

5. The ocean floor that is part of the shore zone is called the

_____.

Choose one feature of the ocean floor that was created by Earth's shifting plates.

Explain how it came to be. _____

_____

_____

_____

Name _____

Date _____

Recognize Vocabulary

Fill in the blanks to spell the term defined by the clue. Unscramble
the circled letters to make the word given by the hint at the bottom
of the page.

water cycle	evaporation	condensation
precipitation	wave	storm surge
tide	deep ocean current	surface current

1. up-and-down movement of water particles __ __ __ __

2. water that falls out of the air in the form of rain, snow, sleet, or hail

__ __ __ __ __ __ __Ⓞ__ __ __ __

3. daily change in the local water level of the ocean __Ⓞ__ __

4. constant recycling of water on Earth

__ __ __ __ __ __Ⓞ__ __ __

5. a series of very large waves __ __ __ __ __ __ __ __ __ __

6. process by which a gas changes to a liquid

__ __ __ __ __ __ __ __Ⓞ__ __

7. river of water that flows in the ocean that forms because of density differences
in ocean water

__ __ __ __ __ __ __ __Ⓞ__ __ __ __ __

8. process by which a liquid changes to a gas

__ __ __Ⓞ__ __ __ __ __ __ __

9. river of water that flows in the ocean that forms because of a steady wind
blowing over the ocean surface

__ __ __Ⓞ__ __ __ __ __ __ __ __ __

Unscramble the letters to form the name of the world's largest ocean.

The _____ Ocean

Use with pages D32–D53.

Name _____

Date _____

Compare and Contrast

The moon's gravity pulls on the ocean and causes tides. The sun's gravity does the same, but because the sun is so far away, its pull is less than half that of the moon. Sometimes, during a new or full moon, when the sun and the moon are lined up, their forces are added together. When this happens, the gravitational pull on tides gets stronger. Write a paragraph that compares and contrasts the effects of the moon's gravity and the sun's gravity on the ocean's tides. Use the Venn diagram below to help you plan your paragraph.

Write About Tides

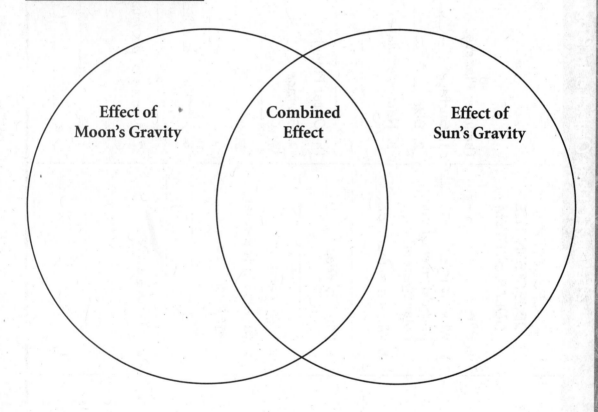

Effect of Moon's Gravity   Combined Effect   Effect of Sun's Gravity

My paragraph: _____

_____

_____

_____

_____

_____

_____

Chapter 3 • Graphic Organizer for Chapter Concepts

Planets and Other Objects in Space

LESSON 1
MOON AND EARTH ORBITS

Moon

1. _____

2. _____

Earth

1. _____

2. _____

3. _____

4. _____

LESSON 2
OBJECTS IN THE SOLAR SYSTEM

The Sun

1. What it is _____ in the center of our solar system

2. What it is made of _____

3. What it does _____

The Solar System

4. Objects in the solar system _____

How Planets Move

5. _____

6. _____

LESSON 3
THE PLANETS

The Inner Planets

1. Surface _____

2. Size _____

3. Names of planets _____

_____

The Outer Planets

4. Surface _____

5. Size _____

6. Moons _____

7. Names of planets _____

_____

Moons and Rings

8. Moons _____

9. Rings _____

LESSON 4
PEOPLE STUDY THE SOLAR SYSTEM

1. _____

2. _____

3. _____

Name _____

Date _____

Investigate Log

Investigate Relative Size

Materials

tennis ball   **basketball**   **meterstick**

Activity Procedure

1 Work with two other students. Two of you should stand side by side. One of these students should hold a tennis ball. The other should hold a basketball. Have the third student stand 3 to 4 meters from the pair and **record** his or her **observations** of the two balls. See Picture A on page D62.

2 Tell the person holding the basketball to move backward until the basketball appears to be the same size as the tennis ball. Use a meterstick to **measure** the distance between the two students. **Record** this distance.

3 Tell the person holding the basketball to continue to move backward until the basketball appears to be smaller than the tennis ball. Again, use the meterstick to **measure** the distance between the two students. **Record** this distance.

Name _____

Draw Conclusions

1. How did the sizes of the balls compare when held side by side?

_____

_____

2. At what distance did the balls appear the same size? _____

_____

_____

3. At what distance did the basketball appear smaller than the tennis ball?

_____

_____

4. The relationship between the sizes of the tennis ball and the basketball is similar to that between the sizes of the moon and the sun. From your **observations,** what can you **infer** about the size of these neighbors in space when viewed from Earth? _____

_____

_____

5. Scientists at Work How could you make sure that your **observations** of two objects show their actual traits? _____

_____

_____

Investigate Further Pluto is the farthest planet from the sun. **Hypothesize** how Pluto would appear when viewed from Earth's surface. _____

_____

_____

_____

Name ______________________________

Date ______________________________

Process Skills Practice

Observing

You have learned that observing is a valuable skill. On the chart below, write what you can see in your classroom from angles other than a front view. Then trade charts with a classmate, and decide whether you both saw the same objects.

Observe Your Classroom

What I see:

Name _____

Date _____

Identify Cause and Effect

Read the selection. Then describe the reasons why the seasons change. Draw a picture that shows what the weather would be like if the sun's rays always fell directly on both hemispheres.

Why Seasons Change

A season is a span of time with a certain level of temperature and a certain kind of weather. Throughout the year, most places on Earth experience changes of season. Seasons change because Earth's axial tilt causes the angle of the sun's rays to change during the year. The Northern Hemisphere is tilted toward the sun for part of the year and away from the sun for another part of the year.

As Earth revolves around the sun, it reaches a point in its orbit at which the axial tilt is neither toward nor away from the sun. This marks the start of the seasons of fall and spring.

Seasons change because _____

_____

Use with page D66.

Name _____

Date _____

Learn About the Moon's and Earth's Orbits

Lesson Concept

The moon orbits Earth. Its movement causes the phases of the moon. Earth revolves around the sun. Its movement and the tilt of its axis cause seasons.

Use the following vocabulary terms to complete each sentence below.

Vocabulary

satellite (D64)	**orbit** (D64)	**phases** (D64)
revolution (D65)	**axis** (D65)	**rotation** (D65)

1. The imaginary line through the center of Earth from pole to pole is its

_____.

2. It takes 365.25 days for Earth to complete its _____ around the sun.

3. The path of the moon around Earth, or Earth around the sun, is called its

_____.

4. Completing one _____ on its axis takes Earth 24 hours.

5. The appearance of the moon, or its _____, depends on the amount of reflected light we see from Earth.

6. Because the moon moves around Earth, the moon is a _____ of Earth.

7. Briefly explain the four phases of the moon. _____

_____

_____

_____

_____

_____

_____

Planet Movement

Materials

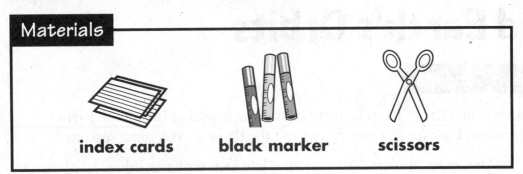

index cards   **black marker**   **scissors**

Activity Procedure

1. Label one of the cards *Sun*. Label each of the other cards with the name of one of the planets shown in the table on the next page.

2. Put all of the cards face down on a table and shuffle them. Have each person choose one card.

3. Use the data table to find out which planet is closest to the sun. Continue **analyzing the data** and **ordering** the cards until you have all the planets in the correct order from the sun.

4. In the gym or outside on a playground, line up in the order you determined in Step 3.

5. If you have a planet card, slowly turn around as you walk at a normal pace around the sun. Be sure to stay in your own path. Do not cross paths with other planets. After everyone has gone around the sun once, **record** your **observations** of the planets and their movements.

Name _____

Planet	Average Distance from the Sun (millions of km)
Earth	150
Jupiter	778
Mars	228
Mercury	58
Neptune	4500

Planet	Average Distance from the Sun (millions of km)
Pluto	5900
Saturn	1429
Uranus	2871
Venus	108

Draw Conclusions

1. The sun and the planets that move around it are called the solar system. What is the order of the planets, starting with the one closest to the sun?

   _____

   _____

2. What did you **observe** about the motion of the planets? _____

   _____

   _____

   _____

3. **Scientists at Work** Why did you need to **make a model** to study how planets

   move around the sun? _____

   _____

   _____

   _____

Investigate Further Look again at the distances listed in the data table. How

could you change your model to make it more accurate? _____

_____

_____

_____

_____

_____

Name _____

Date _____

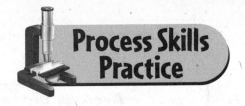

Make a Model

Making a model can help you understand the motion and interactions of objects in the solar system. These objects are difficult to observe directly because of their large sizes and the vast distances between them.

Think About Making a Model

Natalie wanted to make a model to see how the phases of the moon formed. She got a flashlight, a basketball, and a baseball. She asked Rodney to help her with the model. She put the flashlight on a table and turned it on. She cleared away the other furniture from the room and turned off the room lights.
She stood about 6 feet from the flashlight, holding the basketball at waist height. She asked Rodney to stand a few feet away from her. Rodney held the baseball, just above waist height with his arm straight out in front of him. Rodney slowly walked around her, holding the baseball so the flashlight shined on it.

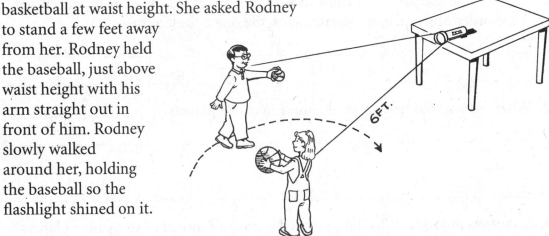

1. What did the flashlight represent in Natalie's model? The basketball?

   The baseball? _____

   _____

2. What do you think Natalie watched as Rodney walked around her? Why?

   _____

   _____

3. What conclusions could Natalie draw about the phases of the moon by observing her model? Try to list at least two possible conclusions.

   _____

   _____

   _____

                                    Use with page D69.

Name _____

Date _____

Reading Skills Practice

Compare and Contrast

Read the selection. Then use some of the signal words to fill in the information about Jupiter and Saturn, comparing and contrasting these two planets.

Outer Planets

The outer planets Jupiter and Saturn are a study in contrast and comparison. Jupiter is the largest of all the planets, and Saturn runs a close second. Jupiter is a cold planet with temperatures dropping to −130°C. But Saturn is even colder, reaching a low of −185°C! Jupiter is 778,400,000 kilometers from the sun, but Saturn is almost twice that distance at 1,423,600,000 kilometers away. Saturn's period of revolution around the sun requires 29 years, but Jupiter cuts the time by more than half, revolving in only 12 years. Even though their revolutions are very different, the period of rotation for each planet is similar; a day on Saturn lasts a little more than ten hours, and a day on Jupiter is a little less than ten hours long.

Jupiter and Saturn are alike in these ways.

_____

_____

_____

_____

Jupiter and Saturn are different in these ways.

_____

_____

_____

_____

_____

_____

_____

Use with page D72.

Name _____

Date _____

How Do Objects Move in the Solar System?

Lesson Concept

The objects in the solar system all revolve around the sun.

Vocabulary

solar system (D70)   **star** (D70)   **planet** (D71)

asteroid (D71)   **comet** (D71)

Label each of the objects in the solar system.

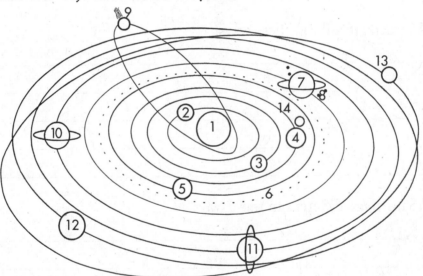

1. _____   8. _____

2. _____   9. _____

3. _____   10. _____

4. _____   11. _____

5. _____   12. _____

6. _____   13. _____

7. _____   14. _____

Name _____

Date _____

Distances Between Planets

Materials

piece of string
about 4 m long

9 different-
colored markers

meterstick

Activity Procedure

1. Use the chart below.
2. At one end of the string, tie three or four knots at the same point to make one large knot. This large knot will stand for the sun in your model.

Planet	Average Distance from the Sun (km)	Average Distance from the Sun (AU)	Scale Distance (cm)	Planet's Diameter (km)	Marker Color
Mercury	58 million	$\frac{4}{10}$	4	4876	
Venus	108 million	$\frac{7}{10}$	7	12,104	
Earth	150 million	1		12,756	
Mars	228 million	2		6794	
Jupiter	778 million	5		142,984	
Saturn	1429 million	10		120,536	
Uranus	2871 million	19		51,118	
Neptune	4500 million	30		49,532	
Pluto	5900 million	39		2274	

3 In the solar system, distances are often measured in astronomical units (AU). One AU equals the average distance from Earth to the sun. In your model, 1 AU will equal 10 cm. Use your meterstick to accurately measure 1 AU from the sun on your model. This point stands for Earth's distance from the sun. Use one of the markers to mark this point on the string. Note in your chart which color you used.

4 Complete the Scale Distance column of the chart. Then measure and mark the position of each planet on the string. Use a different color for each planet, and **record** in your chart the colors you used.

Draw Conclusions

1. In your **model**, how far from the sun is Mercury? _____

How far away is Pluto? _____

2. What advantages can you think of for using AU to measure distances inside the solar system? _____

_____

_____

_____

_____

3. Scientists at Work Explain how it helped to **make a scale model** instead of trying to show actual distances between planets. _____

_____

_____

_____

Investigate Further You can use a calculator to help make other scale models. The chart gives the actual diameters of the planets. Use this scale: Earth's diameter = 1 cm. Find the scale diameters of the other planets by dividing their actual diameters by Earth's diameter. Make a scale drawing showing the diameter of each planet. _____

_____

_____

_____

_____

Name _____

Date _____

Make a Model

Making scale models can help you understand size relationships among different objects.

Think About Making a Model

The table below lists the sizes of some of the different planets and their moons.

Object	Diameter	Object	Diameter
Jupiter	142,800 km	Earth	12,756 km
Ganymede	5270 km	Moon	3484 km
Europa	3275 km	Mars	6794 km
Amalthea	265 km	Deimos	15 km
		Phobos	27 km

1. Compare the diameter of Jupiter with the diameters of its moons. If you were going to make scale models less than 3 meters wide of Jupiter and these three moons, which scale would you choose? Circle your choice.

   A 10 km = 1 cm   **B** 100 km = 1 cm   **C** 1000 km = 1 cm

2. Tell how big each object would be using the scale you chose above.

   Jupiter _____   Europa _____

   Ganymede _____   Amalthea _____

3. Would it work to use the same scale you used for Jupiter for making models of

   Mars and its moons? Why or why not? _____

   _____

   _____

4. Pick a scale from Question 1 for making models of Earth and Earth's moon. Write down your scale and the size each of these objects would be.

   Scale _____

   Earth _____

   Moon _____

Name _____

Date _____

Summarize

Read the selection. Then answer the questions to summarize what you
have learned.

How the Space Shuttle Lifts Off

On April 12, 1981, the space shuttle *Columbia* lifted off for its first flight into
space. The goal of the space program is to explore outer space, and the space
shuttle was the first spacecraft designed to be reused. Despite its complex
appearance, the rockets work according to the third law of motion: *For every
action force, there must be an equal and opposite reaction force.* When a rocket takes
off, the fuel burns, and combustion gases quickly expand and push out the rear, or
toward the ground. As the gases thrust downward, the rocket is pushed in the
opposite direction—upward. The boosters on the space shuttle contain solid fuel,
which feels something like an automobile tire. The solid fuel, along with the main
liquid-fueled engines, ignite to get the shuttle off the ground. After the boosters
are dumped, the main rocket engines continue to burn until orbit is reached.

What law of motion do rockets demonstrate?

_____

_____

_____

How does the space shuttle lift off?

_____

_____

_____

_____

_____

Use with page D77.

What Are the Planets Like?

Lesson Concept

Each planet in our solar system is unique.

Vocabulary

| **inner planets** (D76) | **outer planets** (D78) | **gas giants** (D78) |

Answer the questions about the planets.

1. What are three ways Mercury is like Earth's moon? _____
_____
_____

2. Compare and contrast Venus with Earth. _____
_____
_____

3. Give three facts about the geology of Mars. _____
_____
_____

4. How are Jupiter and Saturn alike and different? _____
_____
_____
_____

5. How are Uranus and Neptune alike and different? _____
_____
_____
_____

6. Which planets are rocky? Which are called the gas giants? _____
_____
_____

Name _____

Date _____

Telescopes

Materials

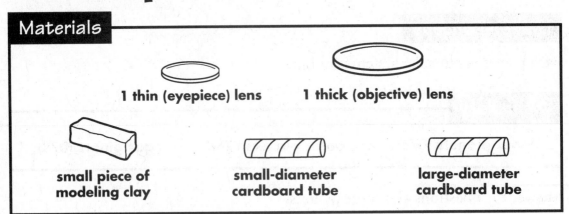

1 thin (eyepiece) lens   1 thick (objective) lens

small piece of modeling clay

small-diameter cardboard tube

large-diameter cardboard tube

CAUTION **Activity Procedure**

1 Press small pieces of clay to the outside of the thin lens. Then put the lens in one end of the small tube. Use enough clay to hold the lens in place, keeping the lens as straight as possible. Be careful not to smear the middle of the lens with clay.

2 Repeat Step 1 using the thick lens and large tube.

3 Slide the open end of the small tube into the larger tube. You have just made a telescope.

4 Hold your telescope up, and look through one lens. Then turn the telescope around, and look through the other lens. **CAUTION** **Never look directly at the sun.** Slide the small tube in and out of the large tube until what you see is in focus, or not blurry. How do objects appear through each lens? **Record** your **observations**.

My observations: _____

_____

_____

Name _____

Draw Conclusions

1. What did you **observe** as you looked through each lens? _____

_____

_____

_____

2. Using your observations, **infer** which lens you should look through to **observe** the stars. Explain your answer. _____

_____

_____

_____

_____

3. Scientists at Work Astronomers (uh•STRAWN•uh•merz) are scientists who study objects in space. Some astronomers use large telescopes with many parts to **observe** objects in space. How would your telescope make observing objects in the night sky easier? _____

_____

_____

_____

_____

Investigate Further Use your telescope to observe the moon at night. Make a list of the details you can see using your telescope that you can't see using only your eyes. _____

_____

_____

_____

_____

_____

Name _____

Date _____

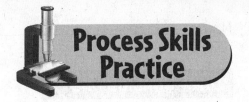

Observe

Telescopes can help you observe details of objects in the solar system.

Think About Observing

Look at the drawings of Jupiter. The larger one was based on a photograph taken through a telescope.

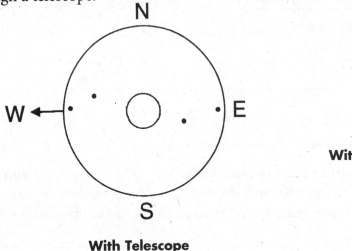

With Telescope

Without Telescope

1. What does Jupiter look like when viewed with the eyes alone?

   _____

2. What does Jupiter look like when viewed through a telescope?

   _____

   _____

3. What features can you see with the telescope that you cannot see without the telescope? List at least two features. _____

   _____

4. The small dots spreading out in a line near Jupiter are the planet's four largest moons. Italian scientist Galileo Galilei was the first person to observe these moons through a telescope. He watched them change position over the course of a few days and inferred that the moons revolved around Jupiter. What do you think Galileo observed that caused him to make this inference?

   _____

   _____

Use with page D83.

Use Reference Sources

Read the selection. Then use reference sources to learn more about the Big Dipper and Ursa Major. Use the information to complete the chart.

The Big Dipper

The constellation Ursa Major, or the Great Bear, contains the group of stars known as the Big Dipper. The handle of the Dipper is the Great Bear's tail, and the Dipper's cup is the Bear's flank.

According to Native American legends, the cup of the Big Dipper is a giant bear and the stars that make up the handle are three warriors chasing the bear. Although the entire constellation can only be seen in very dark skies, the Big Dipper is one of the most recognizable patterns in the northern sky.

Name of Constellation That Contains the Big Dipper	How Constellation Got Its Name	Facts About the Big Dipper

Concept Review

How Do People Study the Solar System?

Lesson Concept

People use different kinds of telescopes, as well as crewed missions and space probes, to study the solar system.

Vocabulary

telescope (D84)	space probe (D88)

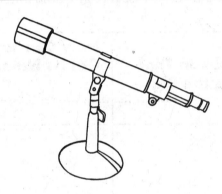

Answer the questions below about how people study the solar system.

1. How are these two telescopes different? _____

_____

_____

2. What kinds of problems occur with optical telescopes? List three ways scientists

have worked around these problems. _____

_____

_____

_____

_____

3. What is the difference between a crewed mission and a space probe?

_____

_____

Recognize Vocabulary

Pretend that your cousins won an exciting vacation through our solar system and beyond. They sent you a letter describing what they saw. For every set of italicized words, write the correct vocabulary term that matches it.

solar system	star	planet	asteroid
comet	orbit	axis	inner planet
outer planet	gas giant	telescope	space probe
constellation	rotate	satellite	

Our tour started close to the sun. The tour guide told us that the sun was really

a _____, *a burning sphere of gases*. After we flew around the sun,

we visited the _____, *the four planets closest to the sun*. We
passed Mercury, which we watched speeding in its *path around the sun*, or its

_____. Did you know that it takes Mercury 59 days to

_____, or *turn around*? We flew on past Venus, which has no

_____, *mass that orbits a planet*. We got a good view of Earth,
and we stopped to look through a _____, *a device that people use
to make distant objects appear closer*. It was traveling around Earth, taking pictures
of stars. After we went past Mars, we flew by some *small rocky objects*, or

_____. Our tour guide told us that we soon would be visiting

the _____, *the five planets farthest from the sun*. She said that

four of these planets are _____, *large spheres composed mostly of
gases*. The first one we saw, Jupiter, was spinning so fast that it looked like a top

turning on *the line running through its center*, its _____. We
went on past Saturn and Uranus. We saw an *object carrying cameras and other
instruments*, called a(n) _____, heading toward Neptune. We

also swung by a(n) _____, *a small mass of dust and ice*. Once we

pass Pluto, we will head toward the _____, or *star pattern*, of

Leo. We hope to see another _____, *a group of objects in space
that move around a central star*. We're searching for different

_____, *large objects that move around stars*.

Name _____

Date _____

Explain

You have been asked to equip a new observatory. The observatory is in an area of low elevation surrounded by large cities. The builders want to know whether to install optical telescopes or radio telescopes. Write a report that tells the type of telescope to use. Defend your choice. Use the outline below to plan your writing.

Explain How Telescopes Work

Telescope chosen:

How it works:

It is the best choice because:

Name _____ Date _____

Chapter 1 • Graphic Organizer for Chapter Concepts

Matter and Its Changes

LESSON 1
STATES OF MATTER

Three States and How They Are Different

1. has a definite shape

2. takes up a definite amount of space

3. particles move back and forth around a point

1. takes the shape of its container

2. takes up a definite amount of space

3. particles slip and slide past each other

1. no definite shape or volume

2. particles move freely and rapidly in all directions

LESSON 2
MEASURING AND COMPARING MATTER

Properties of Matter That Can Be Measured

1. _____

2. _____

3. _____

How Matter Is Measured

1. _____

2. _____

3. _____

LESSON 3
USEFUL PROPERTIES OF MATTER

Useful Properties

1. _____ 2. _____

LESSON 4
PHYSICAL AND CHEMICAL CHANGES

Physical Changes

1. _____

2. _____

3. _____

Chemical Changes

1. _____

2. _____

3. _____

4. _____

Name _____

Date _____

Physical Properties of Matter

Materials

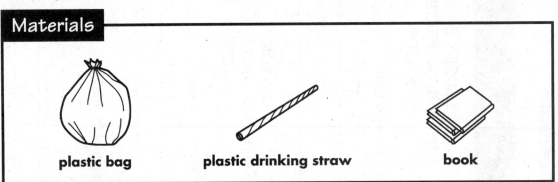

| plastic bag | plastic drinking straw | book |

Activity Procedure

1 Wrap the opening of the plastic bag tightly around the straw. Use your fingers to hold the bag in place.

2 Blow into the straw. **Observe** what happens to the bag.

My observations: _It BLEW up with air_
it got Filled with air

3 Empty the bag. Now place a book on the bag. Again wrap the opening of the bag tightly around the straw and use your fingers to hold the bag in place.

4 **Predict** what will happen when you blow into the straw. Blow into it and **observe** what happens to the book.

My prediction: _Lix ap BOOK_

My observations: _Lift up BOOK_

Name _____

Draw Conclusions

1. What happened to the bag when you blew air into it? _it ᵈ FiLLed_ _up with air_

What happened to the book? _Lift uP book_

_____

2. What property of air caused the effects you observed in Steps 2 and 4?

_____

_____ ? _____

3. **Scientists at Work** Scientists **draw conclusions** after they think carefully about observations and other data they have collected. What data supports your answer to Question 2 above? _Air takes up space_

_____

_____

Investigate Further In a sink, place a filled 1-L bottle on an empty plastic bag. Use a tube connected to a faucet to slowly fill the bag with water. What happens to the bottle when the bag fills with water? _~~cant today~~_

_____

What property of water do you **observe**? _it takes up_ _space._

_____

Name _____

Date _____

Process Skills Practice

Draw Conclusions

You draw conclusions after you collect and analyze data. Your data
should give strong support for the conclusions you draw.

Think About Drawing Conclusions

Gunter measured a cup of water. He poured the water into a small mixing bowl.
Then he poured it into a tall vase. Then he poured it into a pie pan. He was careful
not to spill any of the water as he poured it from one container to another. The
pictures show what the water looked like in each of these containers.

   Next, Gunter poured the water from the pie pan back into the measuring cup.
He noted the level of the water was one cup. He put a half-cup measuring cup in
the pie pan and poured the water into the measuring cup. The water filled the
half-cup measuring cup and spilled over into the pie pan.

1. Based on this experiment, what could Gunter conclude about the shape a
   liquid will take? Give evidence to support this conclusion.

   _____

   _____

   _____

   _____

2. The volume of a substance is the amount of space that the substance takes up.
   What can Gunter conclude about the volume of a liquid, based on this

   experiment? Give evidence to support this conclusion. _____

   _____

   _____

   _____

   _____

   _____

Use with page E5.

Name _____

Date _____

Identify Cause and Effect

Steam Engines

The first engine was a simple steam engine invented in the first century A.D. In the 1760s, James Watt, a British engineer, greatly improved the steam engine, which advanced the development of industry. Watt's engine consists of a large boiler that burns wood or coal, producing heat. The hot air and smoke pass through pipes that run through a water tank. The heat turns the water into steam. The steam passes through a pipe to a cylinder. Inside the cylinder the steam pushes the piston back and forth. The movement of the piston drives the wheels of the engine. Steam and smoke escape through a valve and pour out of the smokestack.

Using the information from the selection above, fill in the chart with the missing parts of the process. Use the words provided in the word box.

produces heat	hot air and smoke	pushes the piston

Cause	Effect
burning wood	
	heats the water
steam	

What Are Three States of Matter?

Lesson Concept

Solids, liquids, and gases are three states of matter.

Vocabulary

matter (E6)　　**mass** (E6)　　**solid** (E6)　　**liquid** (E7)　　**gas** (E8)

What is matter? _____

Fill in the chart below.

Characteristic/ Description	Solid	Liquid	Gas
Has definite shape			
Takes up a definite amount of space			
How particles are arranged			
How particles move			
Cools off to become			
Heats up to become			
Examples			

Density

Materials

 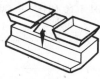

| raisins | pan balance | 3 identical plastic cups | breakfast cereal |

Activity Procedure

1 Fill one cup with raisins. Make sure the raisins fill the cup all the way to the top.

2 Fill another cup with cereal. Make sure the cereal fills the cup all the way to the top.

3 **Observe** the amount of space taken up by the raisins and the cereal.

My observations: _____

_____

4 Adjust the balance so the pans are level. Place one cup on each pan. **Observe** what happens.

My observations: _____

_____

5 Fill the third cup with a mixture of raisins and cereal. **Predict** how the mass of the cup of raisins and cereal will compare with the masses of the cup of raisins and the cup of cereal. Use the balance to check your predictions.

My prediction: _____

_____

_____

Name _____

Draw Conclusions

1. **Compare** the amount of space taken up by the raisins with the space taken up by the cereal. _____

_____

2. Which has more mass, the cup of raisins or the cup of cereal? Explain your answer. _____

_____

_____

3. Which cup has more matter packed into it? Explain your answer.

_____

_____

_____

_____

4. **Scientists at Work** It is important to know the starting place when you measure. What would happen if you **measured** without making the balance pans equal? Explain your answer. _____

_____

_____

_____

Investigate Further Write step-by-step directions to **compare** the masses of any two materials and the space they take up. Exchange sets of directions with a classmate. Test the directions and suggest revisions. _____

_____

_____

_____

_____

_____

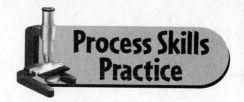

Process Skills Practice

Measure

Measuring involves making observations using numbers. When you use tools, such as balances, to measure, you need to make sure the tools work properly.

Think About Measuring

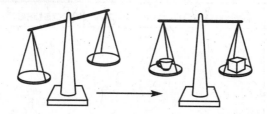

1. Do the cup and the block have the same mass? Explain how you decided.

_____

_____

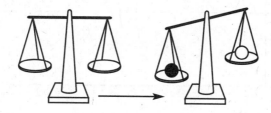

2. Do the dark ball and the light ball have the same mass? Explain how you

decided. _____

_____

Angela wanted to measure the mass and the space taken up by two different liquids. She took two measuring cups and poured a half cup of one liquid in one cup and a half cup of the other liquid in the second cup. She leveled the balance pans and placed one cup on one balance pan and the second cup on the second balance pan.

3. Do the liquids take up the same amount of space? _____

4. Do the liquids have the same amount of mass? _____

Reading Skills Practice

Summarize and Paraphrase

Measuring Mass

Fill in the chart below by defining the three states of matter and identifying how each is measured. Then write a paragraph summarizing the information.

	Definition and How Measured
Solid	
Liquid	
Gas	

Summary

_____

_____

_____

_____

_____

_____

Name _____

Date _____

How Can Matter Be Measured and Compared?

Lesson Concept

An object's mass, volume, and density tell you how much matter it has.

Vocabulary

volume (E13)	density (E14)

Use the illustrations below to help you answer the questions.

A. graduate

B. calculator

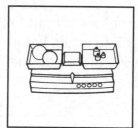
C. balance

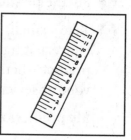
D. ruler

1. Which tool would you use to measure mass? Explain how to use the tool.

   _____

   _____

   _____

2. Which tool would you use to measure a liquid's volume? Explain how to use the tool. _____

   _____

3. Which tool would you use to measure the volume of a solid with a regular shape, such as a box? Explain how to use the tool. _____

   _____

4. Once you know an object's mass and volume, which tool would you use to find its density? Explain how to use the tool. _____

   _____

Use with page E15.

Floating and Sinking

Materials

| plastic shoe box | sheet of aluminum foil | water | modeling clay |

Activity Procedure

1 Fill the plastic shoe box halfway with water.

2 Take a small sheet of aluminum foil about 10 cm long and 10 cm wide. Squeeze it tightly into a ball. Before placing the ball in the shoe box, **predict** whether it will sink or float. Test your prediction, and **record** your **observations**.

My prediction: _____

My observations: _____

3 Take a thin piece of modeling clay about 10 cm long and 10 cm wide. Squeeze it tightly into a ball. Place the ball in the shoe box. **Observe** whether it sinks or floats.

My observations: _____

4 Uncurl the foil. Use it to make a boat. Before placing the boat on the water, **predict** whether it will sink or float. Test your prediction, and **record** your **observations**.

My prediction: _____

My observations: _____

5 Make a boat out of the modeling clay. Before placing the boat on the water, **predict** whether it will sink or float. Test your prediction, and **record** your **observations**.

My prediction: _____

My observations: _____

Name _____

Draw Conclusions

1. Which objects floated? _____

_____

_____

_____

Which objects sank? _____

2. Which do you think has the greater density, the ball of aluminum foil or the ball of modeling clay? Explain. _____

_____

_____

_____

_____

3. Scientists at Work Scientists often look at two situations in which everything is the same except for one property. What property was the same in Step 3 as in Step 5? _____

_____

What property was different in Step 3 and Step 5? _____

_____

_____

What can you **infer** about how that difference changed the results?

_____

_____

_____

Investigate Further How fast do you think each boat would sink if you put a hole in the bottom of it? **Form a hypothesis** about how the size and material of a boat affect its rate of sinking. Then plan and conduct an experiment to test your hypothesis. Be sure to control, or keep the same, all the variables except the one you are changing and the one you are observing. _____

_____

_____

_____

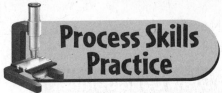

Infer

When you infer, you sometimes use observations or data from an
experiment as a basis for your inferences.

Think About Inferring

Anthony compared how much water different objects displaced, the objects'
masses, the masses of the water displaced, and whether the objects floated or sank.
The table below shows the data he collected. For the experiment, Anthony
assumed that the water had a density of 1 g/cm^3.

Object	Mass of Object	Volume of Water Displaced	Mass of Water Displaced	Whether Object Floated or Sank
Barrette (plastic)	3 g	4 cm^3	4 g	Floated
Marble	28 g	10 cm^3	10 g	Sank
Orange peel	9 g	9 cm^3	9 g	Floated

1. Anthony measured the mass of each object and the volume of water that each
   object displaced. How do you think Anthony figured out the mass of the water

   displaced? _____

   _____

2. Based on the data in the table, would you infer that a metal clip that has a mass
   of 25 g and displaces 6 cm^3 of water would float or sink? Explain your answer.

   _____

   _____

   _____

3. Would you infer that 10 g of cereal in a small plastic bag that displaces 10 cm^3
   of water would float or sink? Explain your answer based on the data in the

   table. _____

   _____

   _____

Use with page E17.

Name _____

Date _____

Arrange Events in Sequence

Scuba Diving

These are events that allow a person to scuba dive.

- A belt is filled with lead weights.
- The diver puts on a face mask, wet suit, weighted belt, and swim fins.
- Tanks full of air are strapped to the diver's back.
- The diver jumps into deep water.
- The diver breathes through the mouthpiece while underwater.
- Tanks are filled with air.

Arrange the events in sequence.

1. _____

2. _____

3. _____

4. _____

5. _____

6. _____

Concept Review

What Are Some Useful Properties of Matter?

Lesson Concept

When solids interact with liquids, the solids may or may not dissolve; solids, liquids, and gases can float or sink in other liquids or gases.

Vocabulary

solution (E18)　　**dissolve** (E19)　　**solubility** (E19)　　**buoyancy** (E20)

Answer the questions below.

1. Circle from the list below the materials that dissolve in water.

   sand　　　sugar　　　salt　　　food coloring　　　plastic

2. What happens when a solid dissolves in a liquid? _____
   _____

3. What is solubility? _____
   _____

4. What is buoyancy? _____

5. Circle the things that sink in water.

   pine wood　　　lead weight　　　sand　　　oil　　　maple syrup　　　air

6. Why do the circled objects in Question 5 sink in water? _____
   _____

7. Why do the uncircled objects in Question 5 float? _____
   _____

8. How can you make something that sinks float? _____
   _____

9. How can you make something that floats sink? _____

Changes in a Penny

Materials

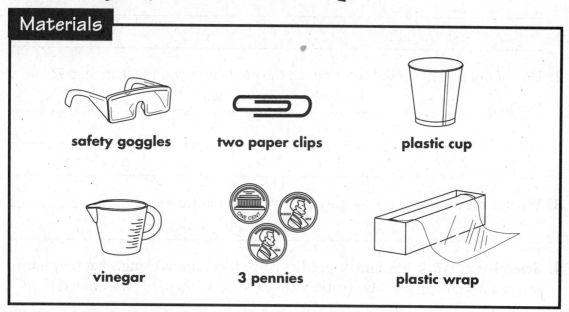

safety goggles   two paper clips   plastic cup

vinegar   3 pennies   plastic wrap

Activity Procedure

1 **CAUTION** **Put on the safety goggles.** Make a coin holder. Bend the paper clip into the shape shown in Picture A on page E25.

2 Place one penny flat on the bottom of the cup at one side. Use the second paper clip to attach a penny to the top of the coin holder. Put the coin holder on the bottom of the plastic cup.

3 Carefully pour vinegar down the side of the cup until the flat penny is just covered. The vinegar should be about 1 cm deep at most. See Picture B on page E25.

4 Cover the cup tightly with a piece of plastic wrap. Lay the third penny on top of the plastic wrap. Place the cup where it will not be bumped or spilled.

5 **Observe** each penny carefully. **Record** your observations.

6 **Observe** each penny after four hours. **Record** your observations.

7 **Predict** what will happen to each penny after one day.

8 Test your prediction and **record** your observations.

Name _____

Draw Conclusions

1. Compare your observations of the pennies in Steps 5 and 6. _____

_____

_____

2. Do your observations in Step 8 match the prediction you made in Step 7?

Explain. _____

_____

_____

3. What is the purpose of the penny on top of the plastic wrap? _____

_____

4. Scientists at Work   Scientists **predict** new observations using what they have
learned from their past observations. Explain how you used past observations

to make your prediction in Step 7. _____

_____

_____

_____

Investigate Further   What will happen if the pennies are replaced by dimes?
Form a hypothesis about the effect of vinegar on dimes. Then **design and
conduct an experiment** to test your hypothesis. _____

_____

_____

Name _____

Date _____

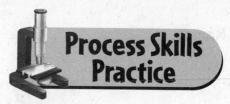

Observe and Compare

Place a penny on a piece of aluminum foil in a glass. Then fill the glass with water. In Box A draw what the aluminum foil looks like.

Check the glass before leaving for the day and when you come in the next morning. What has happened to the aluminum foil? In Box B draw what the aluminum foil looked like the next morning.

Box A	Box B

What do you predict will happen over the next few days? _____

_____

_____

Name _____

Date _____

Identify Supporting Facts and Details

Baking Bread

Bread is the product of baking a mixture of flour, water, salt, yeast, and other ingredients. The basic process is to <u>mix ingredients</u> until the flour is converted into a stiff dough and then to <u>bake</u> the dough into a loaf.

The procedure for baking bread involves preparing the yeast by mixing it with water. Combine the dry ingredients together in a large bowl. <u>Break the eggs</u> and add gradually. Finally, add the liquid ingredients and <u>knead</u> the dough into a thick batter. Let the dough <u>ferment</u> until double in size. Punch down the dough, and add the rest of the flour and remaining ingredients. Mix to a uniform, smooth shape, and allow the <u>dough to rise</u>.

Use the underlined words in the selection above to fill in the boxes in the chart below.

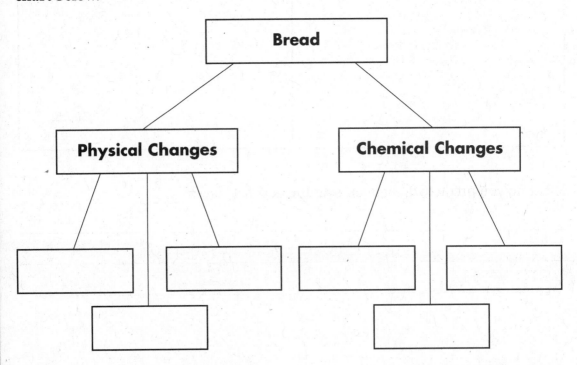

Learn About Physical and Chemical Changes

Lesson Concept

Cutting, folding, and melting are examples of physical changes. New substances are formed during chemical changes. Signs of chemical change include release of energy and change in color.

Use the following vocabulary terms to complete each sentence below.

Vocabulary

physical change (E26)
chemical change (E28)
chemical reaction (E28)

1. If the change produces one or more new substances and possibly releases

   energy, it is a _____

2. Another term for this type of action is _____

3. Changing the shape, size, or state of any substance is a _____

Choose one of the chemical changes discussed in the lesson, and briefly explain how it occurs and what it produces. Why is it a chemical change and not a physical change? _____

_____

_____

_____

Name _____

Date _____

Recognize Vocabulary

Use the clues to fill in the word puzzle with the terms in the box.

matter	mass	solid
liquid	gas	volume
density	solution	dissolve
solubility	buoyancy	

Across

2. different particles of matter mixed evenly

3. salt will ____ in water to form a solution

5. matter that takes the shape of its container and takes up a definite amount of space

8. the ability of matter to float in a liquid or gas

9. matter that has a definite shape and takes up a definite amount of space

10. has mass and takes up space

Down

1. matter that has no definite shape and takes up no definite amount of space

2. the amount of a material that will dissolve in another material

4. the amount of space that matter takes up

6. the amount of matter compared to the space it takes up

7. the amount of matter something contains

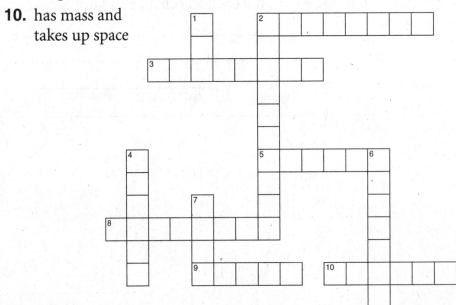

Use with pages E4–E31.

Write About an Invention

Informative Writing–Explanation

Imagine that scuba divers are tired of using belts weighted with lead. Invent a new way for divers to control their buoyancy. Draw your invention in the space below. Write an instruction sheet for your invention. Use the outline to plan your writing.

Name of invention

Explanation of why it works

How divers should use it

Why your invention is better than a weighted dive belt

Chapter 2 • Graphic Organizer for Chapter Concepts

Heat—Energy on the Move

LESSON 1
UNDERSTANDING THERMAL ENERGY

What It Is _____

How It's Measured _____

What Happens When Thermal Energy Is Added to Matter
_____

What Happens When Thermal Energy Is Taken Away
_____

LESSON 2
TRANSFERRING THERMAL ENERGY

The process of transferring thermal energy is _____

Three Ways Thermal Energy Can Be Transferred

1. _____
_____

2. _____
_____

3. _____
_____

LESSON 3
PRODUCING AND USING THERMAL ENERGY

How Thermal Energy Is Produced

1. _____

2. _____

How Thermal Energy Is Used

1. _____

2. _____

3. _____

Changes in a Heated Ballon

Materials

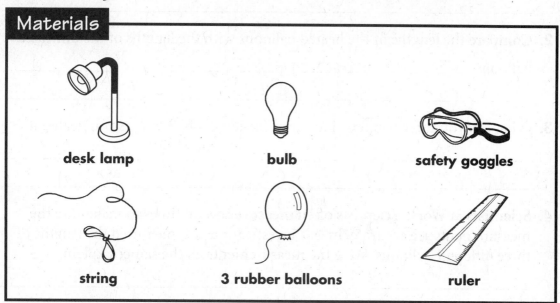

desk lamp   bulb   safety goggles

string   3 rubber balloons   ruler

Activity Procedure

1 Turn on the lamp, and let the light bulb get warm.

2 **CAUTION** **Put on your safety goggles.** Blow up a rubber balloon just enough to stretch it. Tie the end.

3 **Measure** the length of the balloon with the ruler. **Record** the measurement.

My measurement: _____

4 Carefully hold the balloon by its tied end about 3 cm above the lamp. Hold it there for two minutes. **CAUTION** **The light bulb is hot. Do not touch it with your hands or with the balloon. Observe** what happens to the balloon. **Record** your observations.

5 **Measure** the length of the balloon while it is still over the lamp. **Record** the measurement.

My measurement: _____

6 Repeat Steps 2 through 5 using a new balloon each time.

Name _____

Draw Conclusions

1. What did you **observe** as you warmed the balloons? _____

_____

2. **Compare** the lengths of the heated balloons with the lengths of the unheated balloons. _____

_____

3. What can you **infer** happened to the air inside the balloons as you heated it?

_____

_____

4. **Scientists at Work** Scientists often **measure** several times to make sure the measurements are accurate. In this investigation you measured the lengths of three different balloons. Were the measurements all the same? Explain.

_____

_____

_____

_____

_____

Investigate Further Fill a balloon with water that is at room temperature. Put the balloon on a desk and **measure** its length. Heat the balloon by putting it in a bowl of hot tap water for 15 minutes. Take the balloon out of the bowl and measure its length. **Compare** these lengths with the lengths you measured with the air-filled balloons in the investigation. _____

_____

Name _____

Date _____

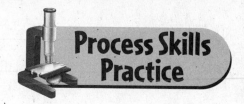

Measure

Making careful measurements can help you find useful patterns in data.

Think About Measuring

The staff at a construction supply store noticed changes in some of the materials at different seasons. They decided to take careful measurements and record what they learned. Their data is presented in the table below.

Material	Length (in meters) at ⁻15°C	Length (in meters) at 10°C	Length (in meters) at 35°C
Brass piping	19.991	20.000	20.010
Copper wire	99.958	100.000	100.040
Plate glass	11.997	12.000	12.003
Rubber matting	49.990	50.000	50.100
Steel beam	9.9973	10.000	10.003

1. What trends do these measurements of different materials show?

   _____

   _____

2. Do you think it would be easy to measure changes to kilometer-long lengths of copper cable during hot summer weather? Explain. _____

   _____

   _____

   _____

3. Based on this data, what would you expect to happen to the meter-square rubber mats under playground equipment during cold winter weather? Do you think it would be easy to measure any changes? Explain. _____

   _____

   _____

Name _____

Date _____

Identify Cause and Effect

Read the paragraph. Answer the questions that follow.

Thermal Energy

Thermal energy is the energy of random motion of an object's particles. The object's average energy of motion can be determined by measuring the object's temperature. As an object's temperature rises, the particles in the object move more quickly. They have more thermal energy. As the temperature of the object drops, the particles move more slowly. They have less thermal energy.

1. When the temperature of an object rises, do the particles in the object move more quickly or more slowly? _____

2. When the particles in an object move more slowly, does the object have more or less thermal energy? _____

Use the information in the paragraph above to complete the chart.

Cause	Effect
	Frost on the window melts.
Thermal energy is added to a pan of soup.	
The particles of an object move more rapidly.	

Use with page E44.

Concept Review

How Does Heat Affect Matter?

Lesson Concept

Thermal energy is the energy of motion of particles in matter. Heat is the process of transferring thermal energy.

Vocabulary

thermal energy (E42)   **energy** (E42)   **kinetic energy** (E42)
temperature (E43)

Fill in the blanks.

1. To move, an object requires _____.

2. Particles in matter are always moving. These particles have

   _____.

3. The particles in a hot object move _____ than those in a colder object.

4. A measure of the average thermal energy of the particles moving in matter is

   called _____.

5. The instrument used to measure average thermal energy is a

   _____.

6. When you _____ thermal energy to an object, the object's particles move faster.

7. If you add enough thermal energy, a material may change its

   _____.

8. Two objects may have the same temperature, but they will not have the same amounts of thermal energy unless they also have the same amount of

   _____.

9. It would take more thermal energy to heat up a _____

   pan of water than a _____ pan of water.

Hot Air

Materials

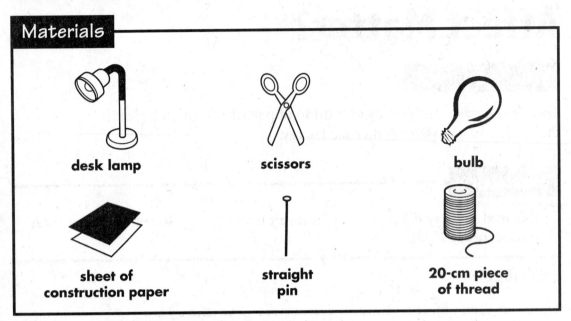

desk lamp

scissors

bulb

sheet of
construction paper

straight
pin

20-cm piece
of thread

Activity Procedure

1. **CAUTION** **Be careful when using scissors.** Cut out a spiral strip about 2 cm wide from the sheet of construction paper.

2. **CAUTION** **Be careful with the pin.** With the pin, carefully make a small hole through the center of the paper spiral. Tie the thread through the hole.

3. Hold the spiral above your head by the thread. Blow upward on it. **Observe** the spiral.

   My observations: _____

4. Carefully hold the spiral a few centimeters above the unlighted desk lamp. **Observe** the spiral.

   My observations: _____

5. Turn on the desk lamp. Let the bulb warm up for a few minutes.

6. Carefully hold the spiral a few centimeters above the lighted desk lamp. **Observe** the spiral.

   My observations: _____

Name _____

Draw Conclusions

1. What did you **observe** in Steps 3, 4, and 6? _____

_____

_____

_____

_____

2. What caused the result you **observed** in Step 3? _____

_____

_____

_____

_____

3. What was different about Steps 4 and 6? _____

_____

_____

_____

_____

4. **Scientists at Work** Scientists often **infer** from **observations** a cause that they can't see directly. What do you think caused the result you observed in Step 6?

_____

_____

_____

_____

Investigate Further Hold the spiral a few centimeters away from the side of the lighted desk lamp. **Observe** the spiral. What can you **infer** from your observation?

_____

_____

_____

_____

Name _____

Date _____

Process Skills
Practice

Observe and Infer

Observing involves using your senses to collect information; inferring involves using those observations to come up with ideas about what caused the things you observed.

Think About Observing and Inferring

Beth had one helium balloon left from her party. A few days after the party, Beth noticed that the balloon was floating around in the middle of the room. Her father explained that some of the helium in the balloon had been replaced with air. This made the balloon about the same density as air, so it floated. But he didn't explain the strange pattern it followed. The balloon would rise near the radiator and float up toward the ceiling. From there, it would travel near the ceiling to the opposite wall of the room near the window. Then the balloon would sink to the floor. It would travel along the floor until it came close to the radiator, again. There it would rise again and retrace its circular journey.

1. Trace the path that Beth observed the balloon following.

2. What would you infer caused the balloon to move? On what do you base this inference? _____

_____

_____

3. Beth observed that the air near the radiator felt warmer than the air near the window. Use this observation and other experiences you have had to make an inference about how such temperature differences could cause Beth's balloon to move. _____

_____

_____

_____

_____

_____

WB250 Workbook

Use with page E47.

Name _____

Date _____

Use Graphic Sources for Information

Using graphic sources can help you arrange information in ways that will make it easier to remember. Use your knowledge of how thermal energy is transferred to fill in the word webs below. For each type of thermal energy transfer, write one fact in each circle.

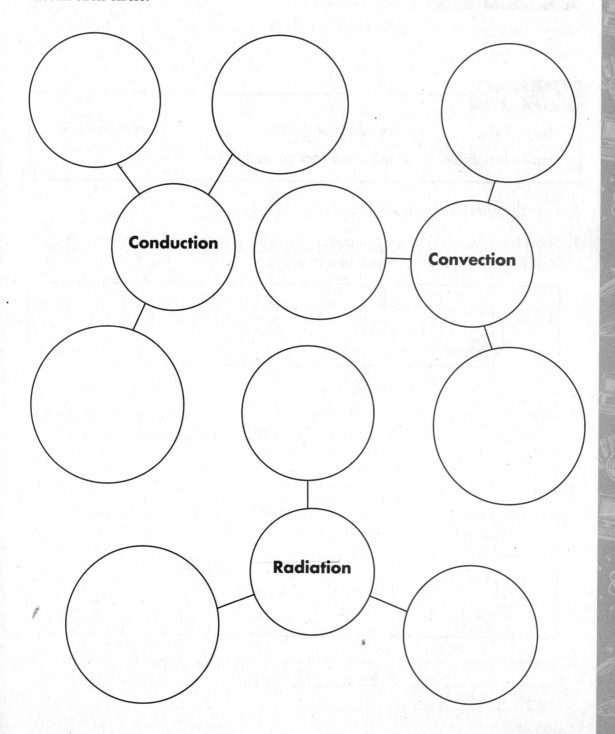

Name _____

Date _____

Concept Review

How Can Thermal Energy Be Transferred?

Lesson Concept

Thermal energy can be transferred in three ways—convection, conduction, and radiation.

Vocabulary

heat (E48)   conduction (E49)   convection (E50)

radiation (E52)   infrared radiation (E52)

Answer the questions below about thermal energy.

1. Show how thermal energy can travel through a pot on a stove to the water inside. Write captions for your pictures.

_____   _____   _____
_____   _____   _____
_____   _____   _____
_____   _____   _____

2. Show how thermal energy can travel from the sun through outer space to Earth. Write captions for your pictures.

_____   _____   _____
_____   _____   _____

Use with page E53.

Temperatures in a Solar Cooker

Materials

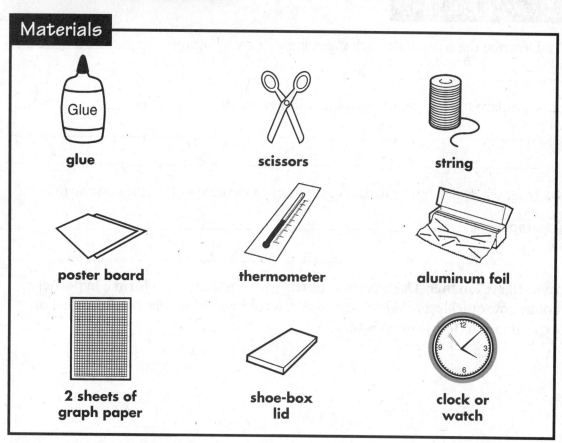

glue

scissors

string

poster board

thermometer

aluminum foil

2 sheets of
graph paper

shoe-box
lid

clock or
watch

CAUTION

Activity Procedure

1. Label the two sheets of graph paper like the one shown on page E55.

2. Place the thermometer in the shoe-box lid.

3. Place the lid in sunlight. **Record** the temperature immediately. Then record the temperature each minute for 10 minutes.

4. In the shade, remove the thermometer from the shoe-box lid.

5. Cut a rectangle of poster board 10 cm by 30 cm. Glue foil to one side. Let the glue dry for 10 minutes.

6. **CAUTION** **Be careful when using scissors.** Use scissors to punch a hole about 2 cm from each end of the rectangle. Make a curved reflector by drawing the poster board ends toward each other with string until they are about 20 cm apart. Tie the string.

7 Put the curved reflector in the shoe-box lid. Put the thermometer in the center of the curve. Repeat Step 3.

8 Make a line graph of the measurements in Step 3. Make another line graph of the measurements in Step 7.

Draw Conclusions

1. Describe the temperature changes shown on each graph. _____

_____

2. **Compare** the temperature changes shown on the two graphs. _____

_____

_____

3. **Infer** what may have caused the differences in the temperatures on the two

graphs. _____

_____

Investigate Further Use what you observed in the activity to **form a hypothesis** about how quickly a different size cooker would warm up. **Plan and conduct an experiment** to test your hypothesis.

Name _____

Date _____

Interpret Data

Interpreting data involves looking at data closely and finding
relationships or patterns in the data.

Think About Interpreting Data

Gertrude made a solar oven. She used it to cook several different
foods. She kept track of the cooking times with the solar oven and
compared them with the cooking times for the same foods in a
conventional oven. The graph below shows her results.

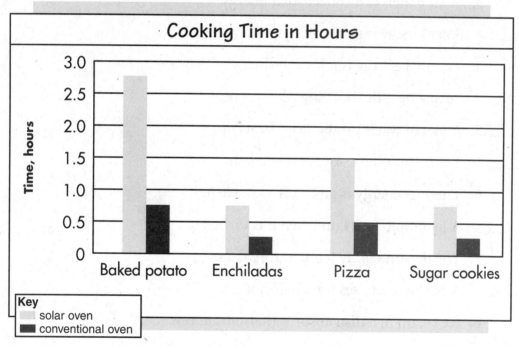

1. How long did it take Gertrude's enchiladas to cook in her solar oven? How long
   would they take to cook in a conventional oven? _____

   _____

2. What relationship do you see between the cooking times for a solar oven and
   the cooking times for a conventional oven? _____

   _____

3. How does displaying the data in a bar graph help you interpret the data about
   the cooking times? _____

   _____

Identify Cause and Effect

Read the pairs of statements below. On the line next to each statement, write **C** if the statement is a cause and **E** if the statement is an effect.

_____ **1.** Wood is burned in a fireplace.

_____ Thermal energy is released.

_____ **2.** Carbon dioxide is formed.

_____ Carbon combines with oxygen.

_____ **3.** Solar panels can collect solar energy.

_____ Solar energy is given off by the sun.

_____ **4.** Thermal energy is released when coal is burned.

_____ People near the burning coal feel heat.

_____ **5.** A pan of water on the stove heats up.

_____ The burner on a stove is turned on.

_____ **6.** Thermal energy is given off as waste heat.

_____ A light bulb heats up when it is turned on.

_____ **7.** The person's body temperature rises.

_____ A person exercises for a half-hour.

_____ **8.** Ice cream in a dish absorbs thermal energy.

_____ The ice cream melts.

Concept Review

How Is Thermal Energy Produced and Used?

Lesson Concept

Thermal energy is useful in many ways. It is considered waste heat if it is not used.

Vocabulary

fuel (E56)	**solar energy** (E57)

Fill in the chart about uses of different types of thermal energy.

Method of Producing Energy	Examples of Use of This Energy	Advantages of Producing Energy This Way	Disadvantages of Producing Energy This Way
Burning wood			
Burning coal			
Burning fuel or gasoline			
Focusing solar energy			

Recognize Vocabulary

Write the letter of the choice that best completes the sentence.

1. The ability to cause change in objects or materials is called _____.
   A friction   **B** heat   **C** energy

2. Any material that can burn is _____.
   A carbon   **B** oxygen   **C** a fuel

3. Thermal energy is _____.
   A the energy of the random motion of particles in matter
   B the motion of particles from one part of matter to another
   C the boiling of water

4. The transfer of thermal energy is _____.
   A conduction   **B** heat   **C** convection

5. We call the transfer of thermal energy from particles bumping into each other _____.
   A conduction   **B** convection   **C** radiation

6. We call the transfer of thermal energy as particles in gases or liquids move from one place to another _____.
   A conduction   **B** convection   **C** radiation

7. The transfer of energy through empty space happens by _____.
   A conduction   **B** convection   **C** radiation

8. Bundles of energy that transfer heat through empty space as well as through matter are called _____.
   A solar energy   **B** infrared radiation   **C** light

9. The measure of the average energy of motion in matter is known as _____.
   A solar energy   **B** heat   **C** temperature

10. The energy given off by the sun alone is called _____.
    A solar energy   **B** infrared radiation   **C** thermal energy

Write a Story About the Future

Narrative Writing—Story

Write a story about one day in the future. Imagine that your main character's community runs on solar energy alone. Describe homes, transportation, and communications powered by the sun. Be imaginative, and use descriptive language. Use the story map to help you plan your writing.

Character:	**Setting (Name of future solar community):**
How does the day begin?	
How does the character travel?	
What do home appliances look like?	
How does the day end?	

Chapter 3 • Graphic Organizer for Chapter Concepts

Sound

LESSON 1
UNDERSTANDING SOUND

Causes of Sound _____
_____

Sound Waves Move
1. _____
2. _____

Sound Waves Travel Through
1. _____
2. _____
3. _____

We Hear Sounds with Our _____

The Three Parts of These Organs
1. _____
2. _____
3. _____

LESSON 2
SOUNDS VARY

Loudness Depends On
1. _____
2. _____

Pitch Depends On
1. _____

Pitch Can Be Changed By Changing
1. _____
2. _____

LESSON 3
HOW SOUND TRAVELS

The Speed of Sound in Air Is _____
_____

Sound Waves Can
1. _____
2. _____
3. _____

Sound from a Ruler

Materials

plastic ruler

Activity Procedure

1 Place the ruler on a tabletop. Let 15 to 20 cm stick out over the edge of the table.

2 Hold the ruler tightly against the tabletop with one hand. Use the thumb of your other hand to flick, or strum, the free end of the ruler.

3 **Observe** the ruler with your eyes. **Record** your observations.

My observations: _____

_____

4 Repeat Step 2. **Observe** the ruler with your ears. **Record** your observations.

My observations: _____

_____

5 Flick the ruler harder. **Observe** the results. **Record** your observations.

My observations: _____

_____

6 Change the length of the ruler sticking over the edge of the table, and repeat Steps 2 through 5. **Observe** the results. **Record** your observations.

My observations: _____

_____

Draw Conclusions

1. What did you **observe** in Step 3? _____

2. What did you **observe** in Step 4? _____

3. **Make a hypothesis** to explain what you **observed** in Steps 3 and 4. How could

you test your explanation? _____

_____

4. **Scientists at Work** When scientists want to learn more about an experiment, they change one part of it and **observe** the effect. What did you change in

Step 6? _____

What effect did you observe? _____

Investigate Further Place one ear on the tabletop. Cover the other ear with your hand. Have a partner repeat Steps 1 and 2. What do you **observe**? **Plan and conduct an experiment** to test this **hypothesis**: Sounds are louder if you listen through a solid material than if you listen through air.

_____

_____

_____

Observe

Observing involves using your senses, including hearing and touch, to notice things that occur.

Think About Observing

Miguel decided he wanted to learn how a guitar makes sound. Miguel held a guitar in his lap and plucked the bottom string. He felt the string vibrate and heard it make a sound. Then he plucked the other strings. Each string made a different sound. He noticed each string had a different thickness. The thin strings made high-pitched sounds, and the thick strings made low-pitched sounds.

1. Write in the appropriate boxes the observations Miguel made using his senses of sight, hearing, and touch.

Sight	Hearing	Touch

2. Based on his observations, what hypothesis might Miguel make about how the guitar makes sound? _____

_____

3. What are two ways Miguel might account for the differences he noticed among the sounds the strings made? _____

_____

Name _____

Date _____

Arrange Events in Sequence

The Parts of the Ear and the Sounds They Hear

When you arrange events in sequence, you put the events in the order in which they occur. Put the parts of the ear in order by writing a number beside each picture. Begin with the part of the ear where sound goes first.

Now that you know the parts of the ear, it is important to know how sounds travel through the ear so you can hear. Write a few sentences describing the journey a sound takes once it reaches your ear.

_____

_____

_____

_____

_____

_____

_____

_____

Concept Review

What Is Sound?

Lesson Concept

Sound is made by vibrating objects.

Vocabulary

	amplitude (E72)	wavelength (E72)
sound (E70)	compression (E71)	sound wave (E71)

Answer the questions about sound below.

1. Give a definition of sound. _____

2. What are three ways you can detect sound? _____

_____

Label the diagram, using the words below.

hammer, anvil, stirrup	middle ear	brain	outer ear
area of low pressure	compression	inner ear	eardrum
cochlea	sound wave	amplitude	wavelength

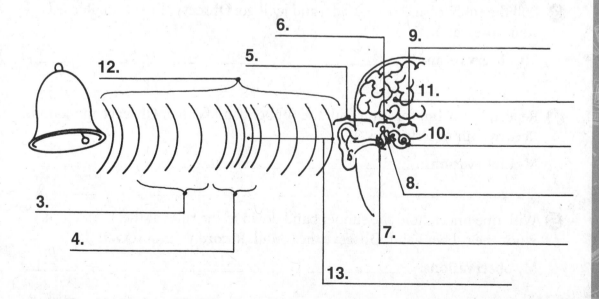

Making Different Sounds

Materials

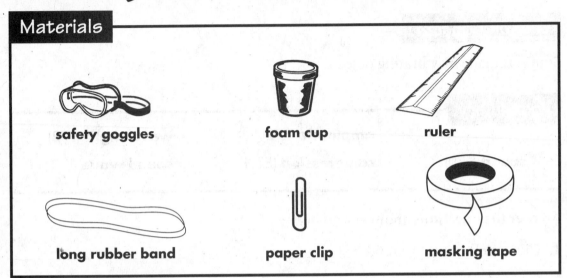

safety goggles   foam cup   ruler

long rubber band   paper clip   masking tape

Activity Procedure

1 **CAUTION** **Put on the safety goggles.** With a pencil, punch a small hole in the bottom of the cup. Thread the rubber band through the paper clip. Put the paper clip inside the cup, and pull the rubber band through the hole.

2 Turn the cup upside down on a table. Stand the ruler on the table next to it, with the 1-cm mark at the top. Tape one side of the cup to the ruler. Pull the rubber band over the top of the ruler, and tape it to the back. See Picture B on page E77.

3 Pull the rubber band to one side, and let it go. **Observe** the sound. **Record** your observations.

My observations: _____

_____

4 Repeat Step 3, but this time pull the rubber band farther. **Observe** the sound. **Record** your observations.

My observations: _____

_____

5 With one finger, hold the rubber band down to the ruler at the 4-cm mark. Pluck the rubber band. **Observe** the sound. **Record** your observations.

My observations: _____

_____

6 Repeat Step 5, but this time hold the rubber band down at the 6-cm mark. Then do this at the 8-cm mark. **Observe** the sounds. **Record** your **observations.**

My observations: _____

_____

Draw Conclusions

1. Compare the sounds you observed in Steps 3 and 4. _____

_____

2. Compare the sounds you observed in Steps 5 and 6. _____

_____

3. When was the vibrating part of the rubber band the shortest?

_____

_____

4. Scientists at Work Scientists use their observations to help them **infer** the causes of different things. Use your observations from Steps 5 and 6 to infer

what caused the differences in the sounds. _____

_____

_____

Investigate Further Try moving your finger up and down the ruler as you pull on the rubber band. Can you play a scale? Can you play a tune? What cause-and-effect relationship do you **observe**? **Form a hypothesis** to explain that relationship. **Plan and conduct an experiment** to test the hypothesis. _____

_____

_____

_____

_____

Name _____

Date _____

Process Skills Practice

Infer

When you infer, you use observations to propose causes for things you observe.

Think About Inferring

Observe each set of pictures, and infer why each instrument makes the sound it does.

A Banjo makes a low sound.

B Banjo with capo makes a higher sound.

1. Infer why the banjo in B sounds as it does. _____

_____

C Harp makes a loud sound.

D Harp makes no sound.

2. Infer why the harp in D makes no sound. _____

_____

Use with page E77.

Compare and Contrast

Sounds of an Instrument

When you compare things, you identify similarities. When you contrast things, you identify differences. Compare and contrast each instrument with the others by putting a check mark [✔] in each box that describes it.

	Piano	Piccolo	Tuba	Trombone
Makes high sounds				
Makes low sounds				
Sound waves close together				
Sound waves far apart				

Name _____

Date _____

Why Do Sounds Differ?

Lesson Concept

Sound can vary in loudness and in pitch.

Vocabulary

loudness (E78)	pitch (E79)

Fill in the table below about how and why sounds differ.

Property of Sound	Definition	Increase It By	Example of Change Using Specific Instrument
Loudness			
Pitch			

Use with page E81.

Name _____

Date _____

Hearing Sounds

Materials

large metal spoon   metal pot   red crayon

Activity Procedure

1 Find a playing field with a scoreboard or building at one end. Use a pencil to make a drawing on the next page of the playing field.

2 Walk out onto the playing field. Use a pencil to record on your drawing where on the playing field you are standing and which way you are facing.

3 Bang the spoon against the pot once. Wait and observe whether or not the sound comes back to you. If the sound comes back to you, use a red crayon to mark that place. See picture A on page E83.

4 Move to another location on the playing field. Again, use a pencil to record where on the playing field you are standing and which way you are facing.

5 Repeat Step 3. If the sound comes back to you, be sure to use a red crayon to mark the spot on your drawing.

6 Move forward and back. Move from side to side. Each time you move, mark your position on your drawing, bang the pot once, and wait to see whether or not the sound comes back to you. Each time use the crayon to mark the places where the sound came back to you.

7 Keep moving to different places on the playing field until you have gathered information from 20 locations.

Draw Conclusions

1. Look at your drawing. How many different positions did you show?

   _____

   At how many different places did the sound come back to you?

   _____

2. Look at all the places marked in red on your drawing. Do they have anything in common? _____

   _____

3. **Scientists at Work** Each mark that you made on your drawing was a piece of data. When scientists do investigations, they **gather and record** as much **data** as they can. All the data helps them draw conclusions. How could you gather more data in an organized way? _____

   _____

   _____

Investigate Further Move to each of the places on the field where you heard the sound come back to you. Blow a whistle loudly in each place. Does the sound come back to you? Describe a simple **experiment** to test this **hypothesis:** Only short, loud sounds come back to you. _____

_____

_____

Name _____

Date _____

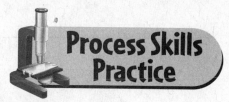

Gather and Record Data

When you gather and record data, you collect information in an organized way so you can use the information.

Think About Gathering and Recording Data

Nicki was interested in echoes. She decided to gather and record as much data as she could about echoes. The table below shows information she recorded over several days.

Date	Location	Echo/No Echo	Observations
June 2	outdoor swimming pool	no echo	playing field and much open space near pool, lots of people in pool
June 2	narrow canyon	loud echo	walls of the canyon with little plant growth, day was hot
June 3	large, empty bathroom	echo	no curtains or shades on window, green shower curtain
June 4	large, empty, carpeted living room	soft echo	thick carpet, no furniture, white walls

1. Do you think Nicki did a good job collecting data? Explain. _____

_____

_____

_____

2. How could Nicki improve her data? _____

_____

_____

3. Where are some other places you think Nicki should collect data? Explain.

_____

_____

_____

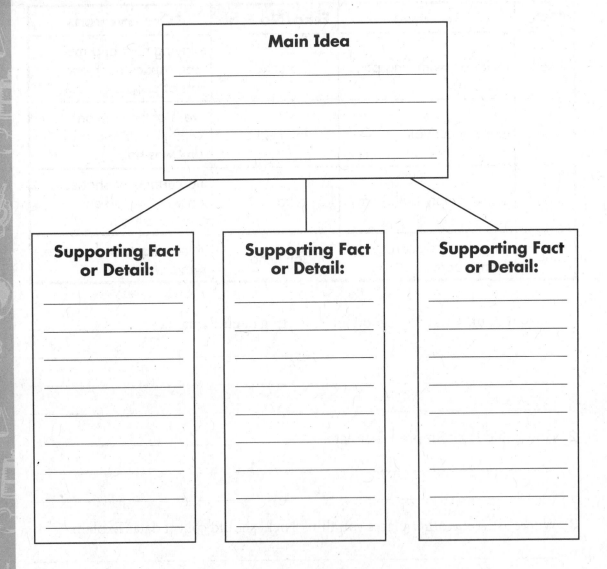

Reading Skills Practice

Identify Supporting Facts and Details

How Dolphins Use Sound

What you read can be more meaningful if you are able to determine the main idea and identify the facts and details that support the main idea. Using what you know about how dolphins use sound, write a main idea and three supporting facts and details.

Main Idea

_____

_____

_____

_____

Supporting Fact or Detail:

_____
_____
_____
_____
_____
_____
_____

Supporting Fact or Detail:

_____
_____
_____
_____
_____
_____
_____

Supporting Fact or Detail:

_____
_____
_____
_____
_____
_____
_____

Concept Review

How Do Sound Waves Travel?

Lesson Concept

The way sound travels affects how we hear sound.

Vocabulary

speed of sound (E84)　　　　**echo** (E86)　　　　**sonic boom** (E88)

Answer the questions below about how sound travels.

1. If you hear a jet flying overhead, where should you look to locate the plane? Why? _____

_____

2. Why do actors in movies who are listening for a train put their ears close to the railroad tracks? _____

_____

_____

3. Why did astronauts who did experiments on the moon communicate with each other using walkie-talkies, even when they were right next to one another?

_____

_____

_____

4. When people build recording studios, they often use soft tiles instead of hard tiles for the ceiling. Why do they do this? _____

_____

5. What causes a sonic boom? _____

_____

_____

_____

Recognize Vocabulary

Match each term in Column B with its meaning in Column A.

sound	speed of sound	sound wave	sonic boom
pitch	compression	echo	loudness
amplitude	wavelength		

Column A

_____ 1. moving areas of high and low pressure

_____ 2. a series of vibrations you can hear

_____ 3. a shock wave produced by an object traveling faster than the speed of sound

_____ 4. a measure of the sound energy reaching your ear

_____ 5. a sound reflection

_____ 6. a measure of how high or low a sound is

_____ 7. the speed at which sound waves travel

_____ 8. an area where air is pushed together

_____ 9. shown by height on a wave diagram

_____ 10. distance from one sound wave compression to the next

Column B

A compression

B echo

C loudness

D pitch

E sonic boom

F sound

G sound waves

H speed of sound

I amplitude

J wavelength

Use with pages E68–E89.

Write a Poem About Sounds

Expressive Writing–Poem

Write a poem about sounds. Include information about sounds that you like and dislike. Use words that make interesting sounds. The word web will help you plan your poem.

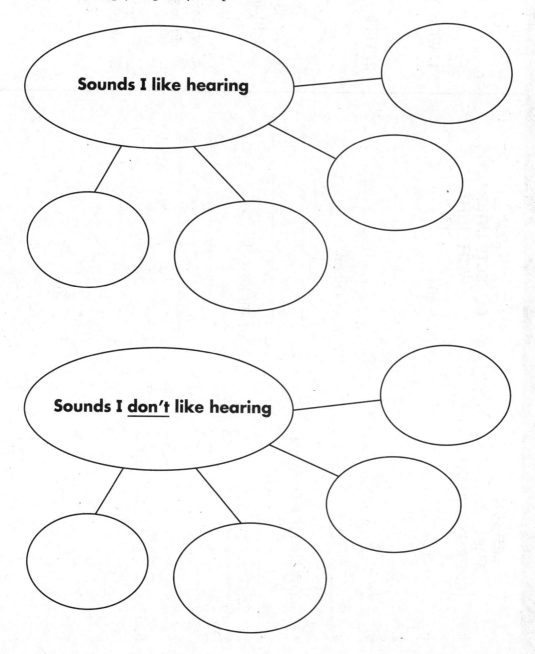

Chapter 4 • Graphic Organizer for Chapter Concepts

Light

LESSON 1
WHAT LIGHT ENERGY CAN DO

1. _____
2. _____
3. _____
4. _____

HOW LIGHT BEHAVES

1. _____
2. _____
3. _____
4. _____
5. _____

HOW OBJECTS INTERACT WITH LIGHT

1. Opaque— _____
   _____

2. Translucent— _____
   _____

3. Transparent— _____
   _____

LESSON 2
WHITE LIGHT AND COLORS

1. White light is _____

2. Visible spectrum is _____
   _____

3. A prism breaks white light into _____
   _____

4. Water drops act like prisms during a rainstorm to make _____
   _____

5. An object's color is _____
   _____

How Light Travels

Materials

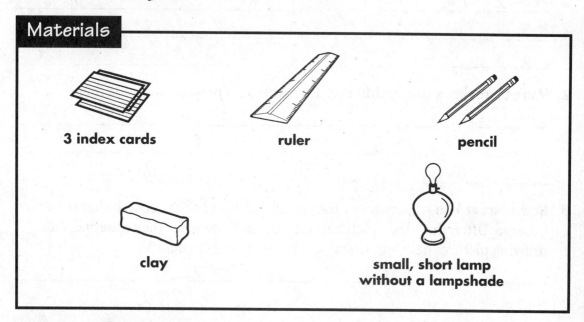

3 index cards   **ruler**   **pencil**

clay   **small, short lamp
without a lampshade**

Activity Procedure

1 Make a large **X** on each card. To draw each line, lay the ruler from one corner of the card to the opposite corner. See Picture A on page E99.

2 On each card, make a hole at the place where the lines of the **X** cross. Use the pencil to make the holes.

3 Use the clay to make a stand for each card. Make sure the holes in the cards are the same height. Stack the cards on top of each other. Line up the edges. Then, hold them tightly together and use a pencil to make sure the holes are the same size and at the same height. See Picture B on page E99.

4 Turn on the light. Look through the holes in the cards. Move the cards around on the table until you can see the light bulb through all three cards at once. You may have to pull down the blinds or dim the room lights to help you see the light bulb. Draw a picture showing where the light is and where the cards are.

5 Move the cards around to new places on the table. Each time you move the cards, draw a picture showing where the cards are. Do not move the light! **Observe** the light through the holes each time.

Name _____

Investigate Log

Draw Conclusions

1. Where were the cards when you were able to see the light?

_____

_____

_____

2. Were there times you couldn't see the light? Where were the cards then?

_____

_____

_____

3. **Scientists at Work** Scientists **observe** carefully and then **record** what they observe. Often they draw pictures to **communicate** what they observe. Did drawing pictures help you describe what you saw? Explain.

_____

_____

_____

_____

Investigate Further Do you **predict** you will get the same results if the cards are at an angle to the lamp? Use the clay to attach the cards to a meterstick. Put a stack of books near the light. Rest the meterstick on books and hold it at an angle to the table. Test your prediction.

Observe and Communicate

When you observe, you use one or more of your senses to learn about something. You communicate your understanding with others.

Think About Observing and Communicating

Jason spent the weekend at his friend Alex's house. Alex gave Jason a flashlight, so that if Jason had to get up at night, he would be able to see. The first night, Jason decided to go down to the kitchen for a drink of water. He turned on the flashlight and started down the hall. Suddenly he observed what looked like another flashlight shining at him. He realized his flashlight was shining in a large mirror. He moved closer to the mirror. The flashlight was shining directly at itself. He observed that the light was reflected straight back. When he moved the flashlight around he observed that the light was no longer reflected straight back in the mirror. In the morning he told Alex about his observations of light. The next night he showed Alex.

1. What was the first observation Jason made about the light from the

   flashlight? _____

   _____

2. What did Jason do when he realized that the light was coming from

   a mirror? _____

3. What was the second observation Jason made? _____

   _____

4. How did Jason communicate his observations? _____

   _____

   _____

Identify Cause and Effect

Read the selection. Use the information to answer the questions about cause and effect.

Luisa's Day

The bright sunlight coming in Luisa's bedroom window woke her up early. Luisa was excited. Today she was going to visit her grandmother. When Luisa arrived at her grandmother's house, her grandmother had a surprise for her. She handed Luisa several packets of seeds. Luisa and her grandmother would plant a garden! Luisa and her grandmother worked all day on the garden. They chose a spot that was not in the shadow of the house. They dug up the soil, and then they planted and watered the seeds. When Luisa went inside that afternoon, she looked in the mirror and noticed that she had gotten a sunburn on her nose. She had forgotten to wear her hat! Luisa's grandmother hugged her goodbye and said, "When you come back, those seeds will have grown into plants!"

1. What effect did light energy entering Luisa's bedroom have?

_____

_____

2. Suppose Luisa and her grandmother had planted their garden in the shadow of the house. What might have happened to the seeds?

_____

_____

3. How could wearing a hat have prevented Luisa from getting a sunburn?

_____

_____

4. What was the effect of light bouncing off the mirror that Luisa looked into?

_____

_____

How Does Light Behave?

Lesson Concept

Light travels in a straight line unless it bumps into something.
When light hits an object it can be bounced off, bent, or absorbed.

Vocabulary

reflection (E102)	**refraction** (E104)	**absorption** (E106)
opaque (E106)	**translucent** (E106)	**transparent** (E106)

Underline the correct answer.

1. You are swimming in a pool. You look down and see that your body looks shorter and fatter than it really is. You realize that the light waves are bending. What is this called?

    A reflection   **B** refraction   **C** absorption

2. Which of the following is an example of refraction?

    A light moving from air to glass   **B** an image in a mirror   **C** an object stopping light

Draw your shadow.

3. In the picture on the left, you are standing in your back yard in the afternoon. Draw your shadow. Then, in the picture on the right, draw your shadow at noon. Put the time of day under your drawings.

Making a Rainbow

Materials

small mirror   clear glass   water   flashlight

Activity Procedure

1 Gently place the mirror into the glass. Slant it up against the side.

2 Fill the glass with water. See Picture A on page E109.

3 Set the glass on a table. Turn out the lights. Make the room as dark as possible.

4 Shine the flashlight into the glass of water. Aim for the mirror. Adjust your aim until the light hits the mirror. If necessary, adjust the mirror in the water. Make sure the mirror is slanted.

5 **Observe** what happens to the light in the glass. Look at the light where it hits the ceiling or the wall. **Record** what you observe. See Picture B on page E109.

Name _____

Draw Conclusions

1. What did the light look like as it went into the glass? _____

   _____

   _____

2. What did the light look like after it came out of the glass? _____

   _____

   _____

3. **Scientists at Work** Scientists **draw conclusions** based on what they **observe**.
   What conclusions can you draw about where color comes from?

   _____

   _____

Investigate Further Change the angles of the mirror and the flashlight. Which
setup gives the best result? Draw a picture of the best arrangement.

   _____

   _____

   _____

Name _____

Date _____

Draw Conclusions

You draw conclusions after you have made observations and gathered data. Conclusions tell what you have learned.

Think About Drawing Conclusions

On a rainy day, Robert put a jar of water on the living room windowsill. He placed a sheet of white paper on the floor. Not very much light came in the window. There was no rainbow on the white paper. Robert drew a conclusion. He wrote it in his notebook. The next day was sunny. Robert did his experiment again. The light passed through the water. A rainbow appeared on the sheet of white paper. Robert wrote down his conclusion about his new experiment.

1. What did Robert observe about his experiment the first time he did it?

   _____

   _____

2. What was different in Robert's experiment the second time he did it?

   _____

3. What do you think Robert's first conclusion might have been?

   _____

   _____

4. What do you think Robert's second conclusion might have been?

   _____

   _____

5. What is your conclusion about why a rainbow formed? _____

   _____

   _____

Use with page E109.

Arrange Events in Sequence

Reorder the statements below to make a paragraph that explains why most grass is green.

The grass absorbs all colors but green.
You see green grass.
Light energy comes from the sun.
The grass reflects the color green.
Your eyes send a signal to your brain.
Light energy from the sun reaches the grass.
Reflected green light reaches your eyes.
Your brain interprets the signal as the color green.

1. _____

2. _____

3. _____

4. _____

5. _____

6. _____

7. _____

8. _____

Concept Review

How Are Light and Color Related?

White light is made up of many colors mixed together. A prism can separate the colors.

Vocabulary

prism (E110)	**visible spectrum** (E110)

Answer each question with one or more complete sentences.

1. What is a prism? _____

2. Explain how a prism works to separate the colors in white light.

_____

_____

_____

3. A prism breaks white light into its colors. What happens if you add

different-colored lights together? _____

4. Sometimes you can see a rainbow during a summer rain when the sun is

out. How does this happen? _____

_____

5. When white light is separated into colors, the colors always appear in the same order. Draw a rainbow that shows the colors and their correct order.

_____

_____

Recognize Vocabulary

Fill in each blank with a vocabulary term.

absorption	reflection	prism	refraction

Dear Jenny,

   Yesterday I did an interesting experiment at home. I held a lamp in front of the mirror. I saw that the light from the lamp moved in a straight line to the mirror. After it hit the mirror, it bounced off. I learned that the word for light bouncing off an object is _____. Then I went outside to feed the fish in the fish pond. I reached into the water to pick up a piece of paper that didn't belong there. When I looked down, it looked as if my arm was in two pieces! I found out that when light passes from air to water, the

light is bent. When light bends, that's called _____.

   This morning in science class, I learned more about light. When light hits something like a wall, the light is stopped and held in. That's called

_____. Then we really had some fun! My teacher brought something to class so we could make rainbows. When white light hit the

_____, each color of light bent at a different angle. The rainbow was great!

                                        Your friend,

                                        Melissa

Answer the question with one or more complete sentences.

The color of an object depends on the reflection and the absorption

of light. How? _____

_____

_____

Name _____

Date _____

Writing Practice

Write a Rainbow Poem

Write a poem that uses the spectrum of colors in the rainbow. Each line of the poem should be about a particular color of light. Use the outline below to help you plan your poem.

Line 1 (Red)

_____

_____

Line 2 (Orange)

_____

_____

Line 3 (Yellow)

_____

_____

Line 4 (Green)

_____

_____

Line 5 (Blue)

_____

_____

Line 6 (Violet)

_____

_____

Chapter 1 • Graphic Organizer for Chapter Concepts

Electricity and Magnetism

LESSON 1
WHAT IS STATIC ELECTRICITY?

Charges that Don't Move

1. Two kinds of charges are _____ and _____.

2. A charge that does not move is called _____.

3. When charges are separated on objects, it is the _____ charges that move.

4. The space around a charged object where electric forces act is _____.

LESSON 2
WHAT IS AN ELECTRIC CURRENT?

Moving Charges

1. The flow of charges is called _____.

2. A _____ is a path for electric current.

3. A _____ adds energy to a circuit. It is also called _____.

4. Charges move freely through _____.

5. Charges don't move easily through _____.

6. The movement of charges is reduced through _____.

7. A _____ circuit has two or more paths for moving charges.

LESSON 3
WHAT IS A MAGNET?

Magnets

1. A magnet attracts material made of _____.

2. Magnetic forces are strongest at a magnet's _____.

3. The space near a magnet where magnetic forces act is called the _____ field.

LESSON 4
WHAT IS AN ELECTROMAGNET?

Electromagnets

1. Current in a wire produces a _____ field around the wire.

2. If you loop the wire around an _____, you make an electromagnet.

3. Two ways to make an electromagnet stronger are _____ and _____.

4. A _____ produces electricity from a magnetic field.

Name _____

Date _____

Balloons Rubbed with Different Materials

Materials

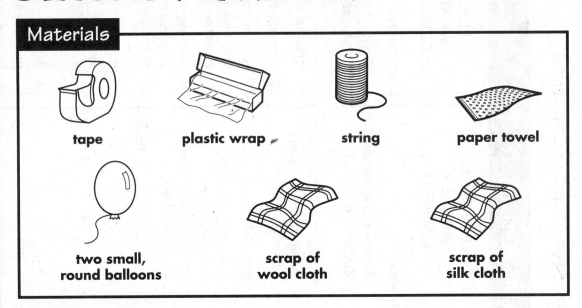

tape   plastic wrap   string   paper towel

two small, round balloons   scrap of wool cloth   scrap of silk cloth

Activity Procedure

1 Blow up the balloons, and tie them closed. Use string and tape to hang one balloon from a shelf or table.

2 Rub the silk all over each balloon. Slowly bring the free balloon near the hanging balloon. **Observe** the hanging balloon. **Record** your observations.

My observations: _____

3 Again rub the silk all over the hanging balloon. Move the silk away. Then slowly bring the silk close to the balloon. **Observe** the hanging balloon, and **record** your observations.

My observations: _____

4 Repeat Steps 2 and 3 separately with the wool, a paper towel, and plastic wrap. **Record** your **observations**.

My observations: _____

5 Rub the silk all over the hanging balloon. Rub the wool all over the free balloon. Slowly bring the free balloon near the hanging balloon. **Observe** the hanging balloon. **Record** your observations.

My observations: _____

Draw Conclusions

1. **Compare** your observations of the two balloons in Step 2 with your observations of a balloon and the material it was rubbed with in Steps 3 and 4.

   _____

   _____

   _____

   _____

2. **Compare** your observations of the hanging balloon in Step 2 with your observations of it in Step 5. _____

   _____

   _____

3. **Scientists at Work** Which of your observations support the **inference** that a force acted on the balloons and materials? Explain your answer.

   _____

   _____

   _____

   _____

Investigate Further When you rubbed the balloons, you caused a charge to build up. Like charges repel. Opposite charges attract. Review your results for each trial. Tell whether the balloons or material had like charges or opposite charges.

   _____

   _____

   _____

Infer

You can use observations of how objects move in relation to one another to infer whether or not the objects have electric charge.

Think About Inferring

On a cold winter day, Lourdes got ready to go to school. She brushed her hair for several minutes. After she brushed her hair, it stuck out and would not lie flat. She walked across the living room carpet and touched the metal doorknob. She got a shock. Her mother explained that her body had built up a charge by walking across the carpet and the shock she experienced was the transfer of that charge to the doorknob.

When she got to school, her teacher did a demonstration with a large, round, metal ball perched on a pedestal. Her teacher called this a Van de Graaff generator. She turned on the generator and asked Lourdes to touch it. Lourdes's hair stuck straight out. Then Lourdes's friend Niles touched her on the shoulder. He felt a shock.

1. Infer why Lourdes's hair stuck out when she combed it. What observations can you use to support this inference? _____

_____

_____

_____

2. Infer why Lourdes's hair stood on end when she touched the Van de Graaff generator. What observations can you use to support this inference?

_____

_____

_____

3. Infer why Niles experienced a shock when he touched Lourdes's shoulder.

_____

_____

Reading Skills Practice

Use Context Clues to Determine/ Confirm Word Meaning

Read the selection. Use context clues to figure out the meanings of the terms in italics. Then use the terms to finish the sentences that follow.

Electric Laundry

Have you ever felt a tiny shock while unloading clothes from a dryer? What you felt was static electricity. When you dry your clothes in a dryer, some clothing gets a *charge*, a number of extra positive or negative particles. When the clothes rub together, negative particles move to and from different items. As a result, some items acquire a *negative charge*, or more negative charges than positive charges, and other items acquire a *positive charge*, or more positive charges than negative charges. The space around an item where electric forces occur, or the *electric field*, attracts items that have opposite charges and repels items that have the same charge. This is why some items of clothing stick together and others do not.

1. A sock that has a positive charge will cling to a shirt

that has a _____.

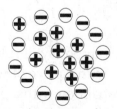

2. The _____ is the space around an item where electric forces occur.

3. Items that have a _____ have extra positive or negative particles.

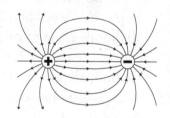

4. A sweater that has a negative charge will cling to pants

that have a _____ .

Name _____

Date _____

What Is Static Electricity?

Objects become electrically charged when they gain or lose negative charges.

Vocabulary

charge (F6)   static electricity (F6)   electric field (F8)

Answer the questions below about static electricity.

1. What is electric charge? _____

_____

2. How can you cause charge to build up on an object? _____

_____

3. What is static electricity and why is this name used? _____

_____

_____

4. Say you rubbed two balloons with a piece of wool and brought the balloons close to one another. Show the charge buildup on the balloons and what the electric field would look like between them.

5. Suppose you rubbed one balloon with a piece of wool and another balloon with a piece of silk and then brought the two balloons close to one another. Show the charge buildup on the balloons and what the electric field would look like between them.

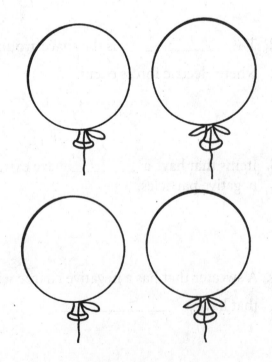

                    Use with page F9.

Making a Bulb Light Up

Materials

D-cell battery

insulated electrical wire

miniature light bulb

masking tape

Activity Procedure

1. Use the chart below to **record** your **observations**.

2. **Predict** a way to arrange the materials you have been given so that the bulb lights up. Make a drawing to **record** your prediction.

3. Test your prediction. **Record** whether or not the bulb lights up.

4. Continue to work with the bulb, the battery, and the wire. Try different arrangements to get the bulb to light. **Record** the results of each try.

Predictions and Observations		
Arrangement of Bulb, Battery, and Wire	**Drawing**	**Observations**

Name _____

Draw Conclusions

1. What did you **observe** about the arrangement of materials when the bulb lighted? _____

   _____

   _____

2. What did you **observe** about the arrangement of materials when the bulb did NOT light? _____

   _____

3. **Scientists at Work** To find out more about bulbs and batteries, you could **plan an investigation** of your own. To do that, you need to decide the following: What question do you want to answer? What materials will you need? How will you use the materials? What will you observe?

   _____

   _____

   _____

Investigate Further Conduct your investigation.

My plan: _____

_____

_____

_____

_____

_____

My results: _____

_____

_____

_____

_____

_____

_____

Name _____

Date _____

Plan a Simple Investigation

You can answer questions about electric circuits by planning and conducting simple investigations.

Think About Planning a Simple Investigation

Jan wants to learn which kinds of batteries will light a medium-sized light bulb like the one in the drawing below. She plans a simple investigation to find out.

1. What materials will Jan need? _____

_____

2. How should Jan set up these materials? _____

_____

_____

_____

3. What should she change in different trials to help her find out what she wants

to learn? _____

_____

4. Make a chart to show how Jan should record her observations.

Identify Cause and Effect

Electric Current Events

Identify the cause and effect in each sentence.

1. A bulb goes out when another bulb is removed from a series circuit.

Cause: _____

Effect: _____

2. When an electrical wire connects a battery to a light bulb, the bulb lights up.

Cause: _____

Effect: _____

For each of the following, write a sentence using the cause and effect that are provided.

3. _____

_____

Cause: a battery died

Effect: a flashlight does not work

4. _____

_____

Cause: a switch was turned on

Effect: a lamp lights up

Name _____

Date _____

What Is an Electric Current?

Lesson Concept

Electric current is a flow of charges through a path called a circuit.

Vocabulary

electric current (F12)	**circuit** (F12)	**electric cell** (F12)
conductor (F13)	**insulator** (F13)	**resistor** (F13)
series circuit (F14)	**parallel circuit** (F14)	

Match each term in Column A with its meaning or its picture in Column B.

Column A

_____ 1. circuit

_____ 2. conductor

_____ 3. electric cell

_____ 4. electric current

_____ 5. insulator

_____ 6. parallel circuit

_____ 7. resistor

_____ 8. series circuit

Column B

A a path made for an electric current

B a material current cannot pass through easily

C a flow of electric charges

D a material that resists but does not stop the flow of current

E a material that current can pass through easily

F   **G**   **H**

9. Label the conductor **A**, the switch **B**, the electric cell **C**, the resistors **D**, and the type of circuit in this diagram. Use arrows to show where the current flows in the diagram.

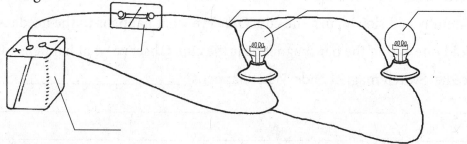

Circuit type: _____

Name _____

Date _____

A Compass

Materials

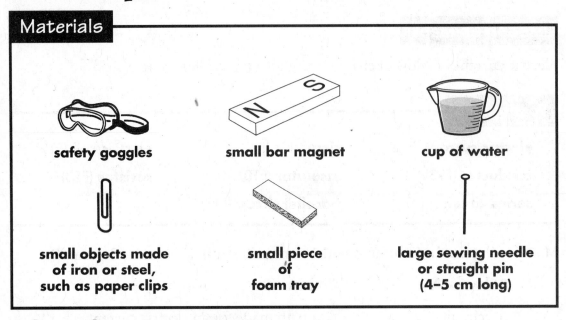

safety goggles   small bar magnet   cup of water

small objects made   small piece   large sewing needle
of iron or steel,   of   or straight pin
such as paper clips   foam tray   (4–5 cm long)

  ## Activity Procedure

1 **CAUTION** **Put on your safety goggles.** Hold the bar magnet near a paper clip. **Observe** what happens. Now hold the needle near the paper clip. Observe what happens.

2 **CAUTION** **Be careful with sharp objects.** Hold the needle by its eye, and drag its entire length over the magnet 20 times, always in the same direction.

3 Repeat Step 1. **Observe** what happens.

4 **CAUTION** **Be careful with sharp objects.** Hold the foam on a flat surface. From one side, slide the needle into the foam with the point away from your fingers.

5 Move the bar magnet at least a meter from the cup. Float the foam in the water. **Observe** what happens to the needle.

6 Carefully and slowly turn the cup. **Observe** what happens to the needle.

7 Hold one end of the bar magnet near the cup. **Observe** what happens to the needle. Switch magnet ends. What happens? _____

_____

_____

Draw Conclusions

1. Describe what happened when you floated the foam with the needle in the water. What happened when you turned the cup? _____

_____

_____

2. What happened when you brought the bar magnet near the floating needle?

_____

_____

_____

3. Scientists at Work What **hypothesis** can you make based on your observations of the needle? _____

_____

_____

_____

What predictions can you make by using your hypothesis? _____

_____

_____

Investigate Further Plan and conduct an experiment to test your hypothesis from Question 3, above.

My plan: _____

_____

_____

My observations: _____

_____

_____

My results: _____

_____

_____

_____

Hypothesize

Making a hypothesis involves using observations to come up
with an explanation that you can test with experiments.

Think About Hypothesizing

Aziz noticed that a strong bar magnet he was playing with attracted a small plastic
car. He could use the magnet to pull the car around on the floor.

1. Based on this observation, what hypothesis might Aziz make about the magnet

and plastic car? _____

_____

_____

2. Pick a hypothesis from Question 1. Describe how Aziz might test this

hypothesis. _____

_____

_____

3. If the hypothesis tested in Question 2 did not turn out to be true, how could
Aziz change it to fit the new information? How could he test his new

hypothesis? _____

_____

_____

_____

_____

Name _____

Date _____

Compare and Contrast

Where Opposites Overlap

Recognizing the similarities and differences between concepts can help you see how ideas are related. Compare and contrast the poles of a magnet by filling in the Venn diagram below.

Differences

Similarities

Differences

North-Seeking Pole

South-Seeking Pole

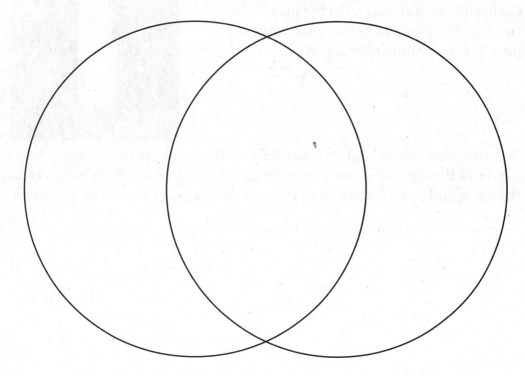

Earth is similar to a magnet. It has magnetic poles. On the lines below, write some similarities between Earth's two poles.

_____

_____

_____

_____

What Is a Magnet?

Lesson Concept

A magnet is an object that attracts certain materials.

Vocabulary

magnet (F18)   **magnetic pole** (F18)   **magnetic field** (F19)

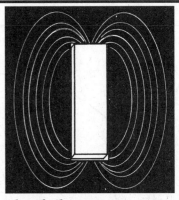

Answer the questions below about magnets.

1. Complete the drawing of the bar magnet by labeling the poles and drawing the magnetic lines of force around the magnet.

2. Describe what would happen if you held up the *S* pole of a bar magnet near the *N* pole of the magnet shown above. In the space below, draw the magnets, label the poles, and show the resulting shape of the magnetic field near the magnets.

   _____

3. How does a compass work to help people tell directions?

   _____

   _____

   _____

   _____

How Magnets and Electricity Can Interact

Materials

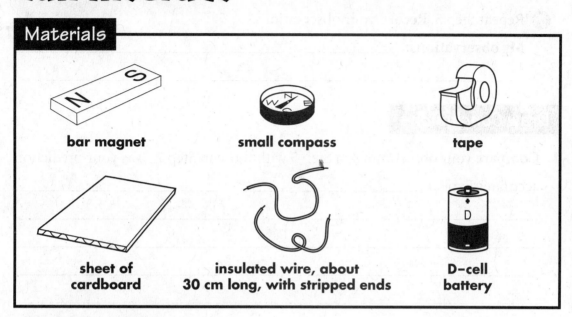

bar magnet

small compass

tape

sheet of cardboard

insulated wire, about 30 cm long, with stripped ends

D-cell battery

Activity Procedure

1 Try several positions of the magnet and compass. **Record** your **observations** of how the magnet affects the compass needle.

My observations: _____

_____

2 Place the compass flat on the cardboard so the needle is lined up with north. Tape the middle third of the insulated wire onto the cardboard in a north-south line.

3 Tape one end of the wire to the flat end of a D-cell battery. Tape the battery to the cardboard.

4 Without moving the cardboard, put the compass on the taped-down part of the wire.

5 Touch the free end of the wire to the (+) end of the battery for a second. **Observe** the compass needle. Repeat this step several more times. **Record** your observations.

My observations: _____

_____

6 Carefully remove a piece of tape.
Place the compass underneath the wire so that both line up along a north-south line. **Predict** what will happen if you repeat Step 5.

My prediction: _____

_____

7 Repeat Step 5. **Record** your observations.

My observations: _____

_____

Draw Conclusions

1. **Compare** your observations in Step 5 with those in Step 7. Was your prediction accurate? Explain. _____

_____

_____

_____

_____

2. Using what you know about compasses in magnetic fields, what can you **infer** about currents in wires? _____

_____

_____

_____

3. **Scientists at Work** Just as you predicted what would happen in Step 7, scientists often **predict** the outcome of an experiment based on their observations and inferences. Based on your observations, what would you predict will happen in the experiment if the current is made to move in the

opposite direction? _____

_____

Investigate Further Test your **prediction**. Remove the battery from the cardboard. Turn it so that its ends are pointing in the opposite direction.

Attach the wire again. **Record** your **observations.** _____

_____

_____

Name _____

Date _____

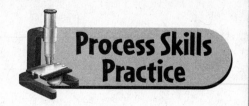

Predict

When you predict, you use what you know from observations you have made in the past to say what you think will happen in an experiment.

Think About Predicting

Gustav was testing the strength of the magnetic field near different magnets. He had a horseshoe magnet, a bar magnet, and a needle that he magnetized using the bar magnet. Gustav predicted that the horseshoe magnet would pick up the most paper clips, and the magnetized needle would pick up the least. After he made his predictions, Gustav tested to see how many paper clips each magnet would pick up.

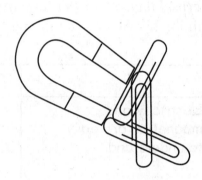

Magnet	Gustav's Prediction of the Number of Paper Clips It Would Pick Up	Actual Number of Paper Clips Picked Up
Horseshoe magnet	30	100
Bar magnet	20	57
Needle magnetized by rubbing it against the bar ten times	2	1

1. The table above shows Gustav's predictions and his results. What was correct about Gustav's predictions? _____

_____

2. Gustav predicted that if he rubbed the needle against the magnet 50 times, he would be able to pick up five paper clips. Do you think this is a good prediction? Explain. _____

_____

3. Gustav tested his prediction, and he found that after rubbing the needle 50 times, it would still pick up only one paper clip. Was your prediction correct?

_____

Use with page F23.

Name _____

Date _____

Distinguish Fact and Opinion

Fact or Feeling?

A fact is a statement that can be proved, and an opinion is a statement that expresses someone's views. Opinion statements can contain the words *possibly, maybe, I thought,* or *I believe.* In the chart below, identify each statement as fact or opinion by placing a check mark in the appropriate column.

	Fact	Opinion
Electricity and magnetism are easy to understand.		
A current in a wire produces a magnetic field around the wire.		
Everybody has fun playing with magnets.		

Write a statement that expresses your opinion about magnets on the lines below.

_____

_____

_____

What Is an Electromagnet?

Lesson Concept

Electricity and magnetism can interact to produce electromagnets.

Vocabulary

electromagnet (F25)

Answer the questions below about electromagnetism.

1. Describe one way to make an electromagnet. _____

_____

_____

2. How is an electromagnet different from a bar magnet? _____

_____

_____

_____

Which picture shows the motor and which shows the generator? Briefly tell how each works.

3. _____

_____

_____

_____

4. _____

_____

_____

_____

Name _____

Date _____

Recognize Vocabulary

Read each sentence below. If the sentence is correct, write *True* on the line. If the sentence is incorrect, write *False* on the line.

_____ 1. Charge is the measure of extra positive or negative particles an object has.

_____ 2. A circuit is a path made for a magnetic field.

_____ 3. Electric current can pass easily through a conductor.

_____ 4. An electric cell supplies energy to move charges through an electric field.

_____ 5. A flow of electromagnets is called an electric current.

_____ 6. An electric field is the space around an object where electric forces occur.

_____ 7. An electromagnet is a wire wrapped around a solid core and connected in a circuit.

_____ 8. An insulator is a material that electric cells cannot pass through.

_____ 9. A magnet attracts certain materials, including plastics.

_____ 10. A magnetic field is the space around an object where magnets form.

_____ 11. Magnetic poles are the ends of a magnet where the magnetic field is strongest.

_____ 12. The current in a parallel circuit travels in only one path.

_____ 13. A resistor is material that increases the flow of electric charges.

_____ 14. The current in a series circuit travels in more than one path.

_____ 15. Static electricity stays on an object.

Use with pages F4–F29.

Write an Adventure Story

Narrative Writing—Story

Write an adventure story about a character who is lost in a deserted area. Have your character use what he or she knows about magnetism to construct a simple compass and find the way home. Use the story map below to help you plan your writing.

Character:	Setting:

How does your story begin?

How does the character make a compass?

How does the character use the compass to find the way home?

How does your story end?

Chapter 2 • Graphic Organizer for Chapter Concepts

Motion—Forces at Work

LESSON 1
MOTION

Definition

_____

Measured as

_____

which involves

_____

LESSON 2
FORCE

Definition

_____

Causes

_____

_____

Measured in

_____

LESSON 3
FORCES IN NATURE

Force   What It Does

1. _____   _____

   _____   _____

2. _____   _____

   _____   _____

Giving Directions

Materials

paper – pencil

Activity Procedure

1 Choose a place in the school, such as a water fountain or an exit door. A person going there should have to make several turns. Tell your teacher the place you chose.

2 After your teacher has approved your place, start walking to it. As you walk, **record** where and how you are moving. For example, you might include the distance you walk, about how long it takes for each part of the trip, where you turn, and any landmarks you use to tell where you are.

My movements: _____

_____

3 Go back to your classroom. On a separate sheet of paper, write directions to the place you chose. Use your notes to add details about time, distance, and position. Don't name the place on the directions page. Give the directions to a classmate and ask him or her to follow them.

4 When your partner comes back, talk about any problems he or she had with your directions. Underline the parts of the directions that caused the problems.

5 Walk with your partner as he or she follows the directions again. Decide together how to make the directions clearer. **Record** the reasons for any changes.

My reasons: _____

_____

6 Switch roles with your partner and repeat Steps 1–6.

Name _____

Draw Conclusions

1. How did your partner know where to start following the directions?

   _____

   _____

   _____

2. How did your partner know how far to walk? _____

   _____

   How did your partner know which direction to walk, and where to turn?

   _____

   _____

3. **Scientists at Work** Directions **communicate** the way to get from one place to another. **Compare** your directions to the procedure of an experiment.

   _____

   _____

   _____

Investigate Further Using your notes and directions, draw a map showing the way to the place you chose. Trade maps with a new partner. Is the map easier to use than written directions? Explain your answer. _____

_____

_____

_____

Name _____

Date _____

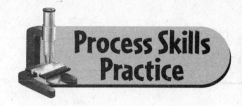

Communicate

When you describe an experiment, you are communicating. Clear communication is important for others to understand your experiment and repeat it.

Think About Communicating

Ann and Carl did an experiment to find the speed of a ball that rolled down a ramp. Ann described their experiment so that Josh could repeat it.

Purpose: To measure the speed of a ball rolling on the floor.

Materials: 3 books, tennis ball, masking tape, stopwatch, meterstick

Procedure:

1. At one end of a long hallway, I used three books to make a ramp.

2. I held the ball at the top of the ramp. Carl took the stopwatch and the masking tape to the other end of the hallway.

3. Carl signaled me and started the stopwatch. I saw the signal and released the ball.

4. Carl observed the ball and stopped the stopwatch when the ball stopped rolling. He marked the ball's position with masking tape.

5. I measured the distance the ball traveled. I divided the distance the ball traveled by the time it took, to figure out the speed of the ball.

Results: The ball traveled 2.65 meters in 7 seconds.
The ball's speed was 0.38 meters per second.

---

1. In describing her experiment, how did Ann divide her report into parts?

   _____

2. What questions should Josh ask Ann about the experiment? _____

   _____

   _____

   _____

3. How would you rewrite parts of Ann's experiment to make the directions

   clearer? _____

   _____

   _____

Use Context Clues to Determine/Confirm Word Meaning

The Rules of Motion

Newton established the law of inertia. This law states that in outer space, where there is no atmosphere and no gravitational pull, an object moving in a straight line will keep going in a straight line. Here on Earth, moving objects are slowed by the force of friction and pulled downward by the force of gravity. For example, when a grasshopper leaps, it does not fly outward in a straight line or fly out into space. Gravity affects the grasshopper's up-and-down motion. Friction with the air affects its forward motion.

Write sentences from the selection that help you determine the meaning of the terms in the sentences below.

Newton established the *law of inertia*.

_____

_____

_____

Here on Earth, moving objects are slowed by the *force of friction* and pulled downward by the *force of gravity*.

_____

_____

_____

Concept Review

What Is Motion?

Lesson Concept

Motion is any change in an object's position.

Vocabulary

position (F40)	**motion** (F40)	**frame of reference** (F41)
relative motion (F41)	**speed** (F42)	

Answer the questions below about motion.

Postcard A

Postcard B

1. Observe Postcard A. Suppose you are the runner looking back. How would you describe the position of the other runner? _____

2. Observe Postcard B. Suppose you are in the crowd, watching the race. How do you know the runners are in motion? _____

    _____

3. What is the frame of reference of Postcard A? How can you tell?

    _____

    _____

4. What is the frame of reference of Postcard B? How can you tell?

    _____

    _____

5. The winner of this race ran 1500 meters in 5 minutes and 22 seconds. What was the winner's speed in m/sec? Show all of your work. _____

    _____

Name _____

Date _____

Pairs of Forces Acting on Objects

Materials

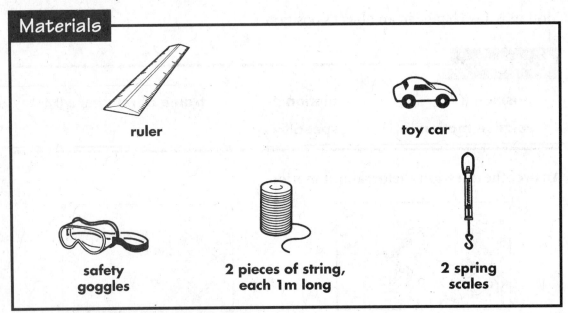

ruler

toy car

safety goggles

2 pieces of string, each 1m long

2 spring scales

Activity Procedure

1 **CAUTION** Wear safety goggles to protect your eyes. **The spring scale hooks or string may slip loose and fly up.** Work with a partner. Tie the ends of each string to the toy car. Pull on the string to make sure it won't come off easily. Attach a spring scale to each loop of string.

2 With a partner, try different ways and directions of pulling on the spring scales attached to the toy car.

3 **Plan a simple investigation.** Your goal is to **describe** how the toy car moves when two spring scales pull it at the same time. Plan to include a chart and a diagram to **record** your data and **observations.**

4 With your partner, carry out the investigation you planned.

Name _____

Investigate Log

Draw Conclusions

1. How did pulling in different directions affect the toy car? _____

_____

_____

_____

2. How did pulling in the same direction affect the toy car? _____

_____

_____

_____

3. **Scientists at Work** Scientists use what they know to help them **plan and conduct investigations**. What knowledge did you use to help you plan and conduct this investigation? _____

_____

_____

Investigate Further What will happen if you pull on the car with a third string and spring scale? **Form a hypothesis** that explains how the three forces interact. Then **plan and conduct an experiment** to test your hypothesis.

_____

_____

_____

_____

_____

_____

Plan and Conduct an Investigation

Planning and conducting an investigation can help you answer
questions about changes in motion.

Think About Planning and Conducting an Investigation

Langston wants to plan and conduct
an investigation that will help him
learn how changing the height of a
ramp affects how a toy car moves.

1. To plan an investigation, Langston first needs to pose a question, starting with
   what he wants to learn. What question do you think Langston should pose?

   _____

   _____

2. Identify what Langston should measure, change, and keep the same to answer
   his question, and how he should do each of these things. What should

   Langston measure? _____

   _____

   What should Langston change? _____

   What should Langston keep the same? _____

   _____

3. Draw or describe in words Langston's investigation. _____

   _____

   _____

   _____

   _____

4. What knowledge did you use to come up with ideas for Langston's

   investigation? _____

   _____

   _____

Reading Skills Practice

Identify Cause and Effect

What Gets Things Moving

Identify the cause and effect in each sentence below.

A cross-country skier gains speed skiing down a small hill.

Cause: **Effect:**
_____

A jogger going up a steep hill slows down.

Cause: **Effect:**
_____

A flag waves as the wind blows.

Cause: **Effect:**
_____

A go-cart stops when it crashes into a tree.

Cause: **Effect:**
_____

A tennis player hits a ball, and it goes over the net.

Cause: **Effect:**
_____

Name _____

Date _____

What Effects Do Forces Have on Objects?

Lesson Concept

Forces can affect how objects move.

Vocabulary

force (F46) **acceleration** (F48) **newton** (F51)

1. Define *force*, and name the unit used to measure forces.

_____

2. Define *acceleration*, and tell how acceleration is related to force.

_____

_____

3. List two ways you can increase acceleration. _____

_____

_____

4. Below are pictures of forces. Use arrows to draw the forces the students are exerting in each picture. The lengths of the arrows should indicate the relative sizes of the forces.

Name _____

Date _____

Forces on a Sliding Box

Materials

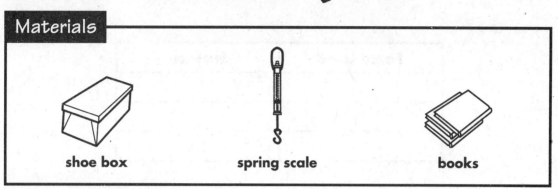

shoe box   spring scale   books

Activity Procedure

1. Use the table below to **record** your **observations**.

2. Put the hook of the spring scale through the two openings on the end of the box. Place several books in the box.

3. Use the spring scale to slowly drag the box across the top of the desk or table. Be sure to pull with the spring scale straight out from the side of the box. Practice this step several times until you can pull the box at a steady, slow speed.

4. When you are ready, **measure** the force of your pull as you drag the box. **Record** the force measurement and the surface on which you dragged the box. **Observe** the texture of the surface.

5. Repeat Steps 3 and 4, dragging the box across other surfaces, such as the classroom floor, carpet, tile, and cement. **Predict** the force needed to drag the box on each surface.

Surface	Predicted Force	Force

Name _____

Draw Conclusions

1. In the table below, list the forces you used in order from the smallest to the largest.

Force Used	Surface

What was the least amount of force you used? _____
_____
_____

2. In your new table, write the name of each surface next to the force you used on it. On which surface did you use the greatest amount of force?
_____
_____

3. How did a surface affect the force needed to drag the shoe box across it?
_____
_____

4. Scientists at Work After scientists gather data, they often put it in some kind of order to help them understand their results. How did putting your data in **order** help you in this investigation? _____
_____

Investigate Further Predict how much force it would take to pull the shoe box across a patch of ice. If possible, find a place and test your prediction.
_____
_____

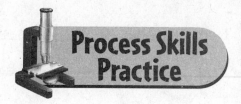

Order

You put data in order when you rank the data from lowest to highest.

Think About Ordering

Jaya read that friction slows moving objects and can make them stop. She tested different materials to see how well each could stop a rolling golf ball. She rolled a set of golf balls, one at a time, down a short ramp onto different surfaces and measured how far they rolled before they stopped. For each of the surfaces, she averaged the distances the golf balls rolled. The table shows her data.

Material	Average Distance
Corrugated cardboard	41 cm
Thin-pile carpet	32 cm
Thick-pile carpet	22 cm
Plastic with small spikes (under-side of carpet protector)	10 cm
Smooth plastic (carpet protector)	115 cm
Carpet pad (carpet side)	52 cm

1. Jaya is trying to find the material that will stop rolling golf balls the fastest. To order the materials she tested from best to worst, should she start with the highest measurement or the lowest measurement? Explain.

   _____

   _____

2. Order the materials from the best material to stop a rolling golf ball to the worst.

Material	Average Distance

Make Generalizations

Skating Over Friction

In the past, ice skating was a means of transportation. Later, skating became a sport. Whether used for transportation or competition, the thin skate blades support all the weight of the skater. Warmth conducted through the metal causes the ice under the blades to melt slightly. The water reduces the friction between the blades and the ice, making it easier for the blades to slide. Speed skates have very long blades to increase speed, and skaters wear thin, clingy bodysuits that reduce drag.

Complete the chart using information found in the selection. Then write a generalization based on the information you gathered.

If a skater . . .	. . . the skater's speed will . . .
wears loose, baggy clothing	
wears a clingy bodysuit	
skates on ice with a thin layer of water on top of it	
skates on ice with no water on top of it	

Generalization:

_____

_____

Concept Review

What Are Some Forces in Nature?

Lesson Concept

Gravity, friction, the electromagnetic force, and the strong nuclear force are some forces in nature.

Vocabulary

gravity (F56)	weight (F57)	friction (F58)

Answer the questions below about forces.

1. Define *gravity,* and write three facts about gravity. _____

_____

_____

_____

_____

2. What is weight? Why does weight vary on different planets? _____

_____

_____

3. What is friction, and how is it useful to you? _____

_____

_____

Recognize Vocabulary

Match each term in Column B with its meaning in Column A.

position	motion	frame of reference
relative motion	speed	force
newton	acceleration	gravity
weight	friction	

Column A

_____ 1. any change of position

_____ 2. the measure of the force of gravity on an object

_____ 3. a push or a pull

_____ 4. a certain place, described in comparison to another place

_____ 5. a change in the speed or direction of an object's motion

_____ 6. the force that keeps objects that are touching each other from sliding past each other easily

_____ 7. all the things around you that you can sense and use to describe motion

_____ 8. the metric unit of force

_____ 9. a measure of an object's change in position during a unit of time

_____ 10. motion described in relation to a frame of reference

_____ 11. a force that pulls objects toward each other

Column B

A acceleration

B force

C frame of reference

D friction

E gravity

F motion

G newton

H position

I relative motion

J speed

K weight

Write a Public Service Announcement

Persuasive Writing–Advocacy

Write a radio public service announcement reminding adults to have their cars' oil changed regularly. Use what you know about the effects of friction on automobile engines to make your point. Use the outline below to help you plan your writing.

State your opinion.

State reasons.
    Reason 1:

    Reason 2:

    Reason 3:

Restate your opinion or call for action.

Chapter 3 • Graphic Organizer for Chapter Concepts

Simple Machines

LESSON 1
SIMPLE MACHINES

Types _____
_____
_____
_____

Lever _____
_____

effort force _____

resulting force _____

Example _____
_____

LESSON 2
SIMPLE MACHINES THAT TURN

Fixed Pulley _____
Description _____
_____
How It Works _____
_____

Movable Pulley _____
Description _____
_____
How It Works _____

Wheel and Axle _____
Description _____
_____
How It Works _____
_____

LESSON 3
INCLINED PLANES

Inclined Plane _____
Description _____
_____
How It Works _____
_____

Screw _____
Description _____
How It Works _____

Wedge _____
Description _____
How It Works _____

Experimenting with a Lever

Materials

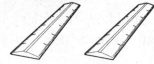

2 wooden rulers   **2 identical rubber bands, long**   **safety goggles**

CAUTION

Activity Procedure

1 **CAUTION** **Put on your safety goggles.** Put a rubber band 2 cm from each end of the ruler. One band should be at the 2-cm mark, and the other should be at the 28-cm mark.

Finger Position	Observations	Length of Rubber Band on 2-cm Mark	Length of Rubber Band on 28-cm Mark
15-cm mark			
17-cm mark			
19-cm mark			
21-cm mark			

② Have a partner lift the ruler by holding the rubber bands. Place your index finger at the 15-cm mark, and press down just enough to stretch the rubber bands. Your partner should lift hard enough on both rubber bands to keep the ruler level.

③ Have a third person use the other ruler to **measure** the lengths of the two bands. **Record** your **observations** and measurements in the chart on WB333.

④ Move your finger to the 17-cm mark. Your partner should keep the ruler level. Again **measure** the length of the rubber bands and **record** your **observations** and measurements.

⑤ Repeat Step 4, this time with your finger at the 19-cm mark and then the 21-cm mark.

Draw Conclusions

1. Describe what happened to the ruler each time you moved your finger away from the center of it. _____

_____

2. **Compare** the ruler and rubber bands to a seesaw. What was the ruler? What were the forces of the rubber bands? _____

_____

_____

3. **Scientists at Work** Look at the **measurements** you recorded. How do they support your other observations? Is there a pattern? _____

_____

_____

Investigate Further For the same ruler setup, **predict** what will happen if you put your finger on the 9-cm mark. Try it and see if your prediction is correct.

_____

_____

Name _____

Date _____

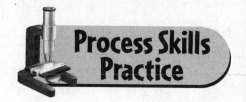
Measure

You measure when you make observations and comparisons using numbers.

Think About Measuring

Below are pictures of people on a seesaw. The bar that holds up the seesaw is called the fulcrum. Use a ruler to measure the distance in centimeters between the fulcrum and each end of the seesaw. Record your measurements in the chart below.

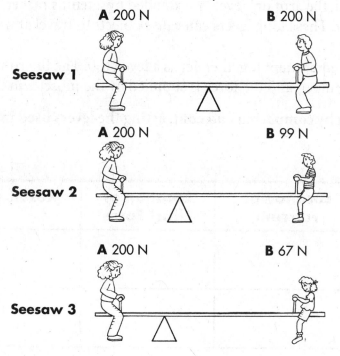

A 200 N   **B** 200 N

Seesaw 1

A 200 N   **B** 99 N

Seesaw 2

A 200 N   **B** 67 N

Seesaw 3

Seesaw	Distance from A to Fulcrum	Weight of A in Newtons	Distance from B to Fulcrum	Weight of B in Newtons
1		200 N		200 N
2		200 N		99 N
3		200 N		67 N

What relationship do you see between the distances of the people from the

fulcrum and the people's weights? _____

_____

Compare and Contrast

Scoring Points with Simple Machines

Levers are often used in sports. Sometimes the lever is your arm, and in other sports, the lever is the equipment the players use.

When you throw a ball, your arm acts as a lever and increases the speed at which the ball moves. In swimming, each arm acts like a long paddle. In tennis, hockey, and baseball, the arm or "lever" is extended by a tennis racket, hockey stick, or baseball bat. These long levers can cause objects to travel at tremendous speeds.

The arm and the equipment together act as a lever, too. The fulcrum may be the elbow or the shoulder, and the force is supplied by the muscles in the arm.

Complete the chart by comparing and contrasting the levers used in different sports.

Type of Sport	Location of Fulcrum	Location of Effort Force	Result of Force
Baseball			
Swimming			
Tennis			
Hockey			

Name _____

Date _____

Concept Review

How Does a Lever Help Us Do Work?

Lesson Concept

A lever is a simple machine that can change the size or direction of a force.

Vocabulary

simple machine (F70)	**lever** (F70)	**fulcrum** (F70)
effort force (F70)	**work** (F74)	

Answer the questions below about levers.

1. What is the scientific definition of work? Write the formula for work.

   _____

For each lever, label the fulcrum and the effort force. Tell how each lever changes force.

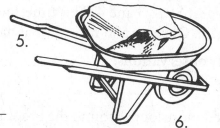

2. _____

3. _____

4. How a crowbar changes force: _____

   _____

5. _____

6. _____

7. How a wheelbarrow changes force:

   _____

   _____

How a Pulley Works

Materials

2 broom handles

strong rope, 6 m or longer

CAUTION ## Activity Procedure

1. Firmly tie one end of the rope to the center of one of the broom handles. This will be Handle 1.

2. Have two people face each other and stand about 30 cm apart. Have one person hold Handle 1. His or her hands should be about 40 cm apart— 20 cm on either side of the rope. Have the other person hold the other broom handle (Handle 2) in the same way.

3. Loop the rope around Handle 2 and back over Handle 1.

4. Stand behind the person holding Handle 1. Have your partners try to hold the broom handles apart while you slowly pull on the free end of the rope. **CAUTION** **Don't let fingers get caught between the handles. Observe** and **record** what happens.

My observations: _____

_____

5. Repeat Steps 3 and 4. This time, loop the rope back around Handles 1 and 2 again. **Observe** and **record** what happens.

My observations: _____

_____

6. Add more loops around the broom handles. Again pull on the free end of the rope to try to bring the handles together. **Observe** and **record** what happens.

My observations: _____

_____

Draw Conclusions

1. **Compare** your observations in Steps 4, 5, and 6. Which way of looping the rope made it hardest to pull the handles together? Which way made it easiest?

   _____

   _____

   _____

2. Reread the description of a pulley in the Activity Purpose. What in this investigation worked as wheels do? _____

   _____

3. **Scientists at Work** How did the handles and rope change your effort force? **Compare** this to how levers work. How is it like levers? How is it different?

   _____

   _____

   _____

   _____

Investigate Further How do you think adding loops of rope will change the way the broom handles and rope work? **Form a hypothesis** that explains how adding rope loops will change your results. **Plan and conduct an experiment** to test your hypothesis. Plan to use a spring scale to mesure forces.

_____

_____

_____

Name _____

Date _____

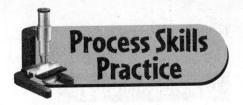

Process Skills Practice

Compare

Comparing involves noticing how things are alike and how they are different.

Think About Comparing

Tyrone looks in his father's toolbox. He notices two different screwdrivers.

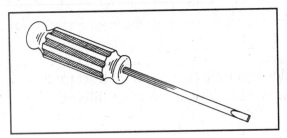

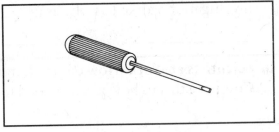

Screwdriver A   **Screwdriver B**

1. How are these tools alike? _____

_____

2. How are these tools different? _____

_____

3. Which screwdriver could Tyrone use to unscrew a door from its hinges?

_____

4. Which screwdriver could Tyrone use to take apart a watch? _____

_____

5. Why couldn't Tyrone switch the tools for the jobs in Questions 3 and 4?

_____

_____

_____

_____

Use with page F77.

Distinguish Fact and Opinion

Building the Pyramids

How did the ancient Egyptians move huge blocks of stone to build the pyramids? You might be surprised to discover that they used simple machines! Scientists believe the Egyptians built spiral ramps that gradually wound around each pyramid, much like a road winding its way up a mountain. A spiral ramp is longer than a ramp that goes directly up the side of a pyramid, but less effort is needed to climb it. Another machine the Egyptians might have used is the roller. The Egyptians probably placed many smooth logs under a heavy block of stone, and then a team of men pulled the stone on the rollers.

Decide which statements below are facts and which are opinions.

_____ The Egyptians did not like using machines to build the pyramids.

_____ Spiral ramps would have been longer than steep ramps.

_____ Pulleys and wedges were used to build the pyramids.

_____ The Egyptians could have used complex machines.

Which opinion statement is most likely to be true?

_____

_____

_____

How Do a Wheel and Axle and a Pulley Help Us Do Work?

Lesson Concept

A wheel and axle and a pulley are simple machines that can change the size or direction of forces.

Vocabulary

pulley (F78)	wheel and axle (F80)

Look at each picture and answer the questions.

1. What kind of simple machine is shown?

_____

2. How does this machine help you do work?

_____

_____

3. What kind of simple machine is shown?

_____

4. How does this machine help you do work?

_____

_____

_____

5. What kind of simple machines are put

together to form this system? _____

_____

_____

6. How does this system help you do work? _____

_____

Name _____

Date _____

Make an Archimedes' Screw

Materials

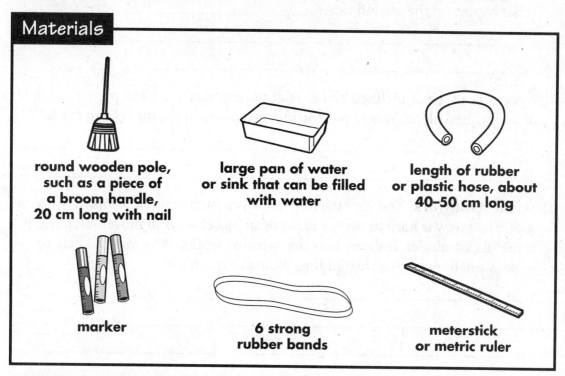

round wooden pole, such as a piece of a broom handle, 20 cm long with nail

large pan of water or sink that can be filled with water

length of rubber or plastic hose, about 40–50 cm long

marker

6 strong rubber bands

meterstick or metric ruler

Activity Procedure

1. Use the meterstick and marker to divide the pole into five equal sections.

2. Use a rubber band to hold the hose to one end of the pole. The band should not be so tight that it closes off the hose, but it should be tight enough to hold the hose in place.

3. Wind the hose around the pole in a spiral so that it passes over your marks. Use a rubber band to hold the top of the hose in place. Put two or three more bands around the hose and pole so that nothing slips. Wiggle the hose around so the ends open at right angles to the length of the pole. You have built an Archimedes' screw.

4. Put the nail end of the Archimedes' screw in the large pan or sink of water so the device rests on the head of the nail and makes a low angle with the bottom of the pan. Make sure both ends of the screw are over the pan. Turn the Archimedes' screw clockwise 12 times. Now turn the screw in the other direction 12 times. **Observe** what happens.

Name _____

Investigate Log

Draw Conclusions

1. What happened when you turned the Archimedes' screw the first time? What happened the second time? _____

   _____

   _____

2. A screw is a type of inclined plane, a flat sloping surface. A ramp is an example of an inclined plane. Where was the inclined plane in the model you made?

   _____

   _____

3. **Scientists at Work** The Archimedes' screw you built is not a completely useful tool. The screw is hard to turn, and there are easier ways to move water. But it is useful as a **model**. It shows how the machine works. Why might it help to make a small model before building a full-size machine?

   _____

   _____

   _____

Investigate Further There are many inclined planes around you. Select one day to see how many ramps and screws you can find at school and at home. Make a list of those you find. Tell how each helps people do work.

_____

_____

_____

_____

_____

_____

Name _____

Date _____

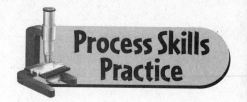

Make a Model

Making a small model of a simple machine can help you investigate ways to improve the real thing.

Think About Making a Model

Jasper was moving from his apartment to a house. He asked his friends to help him move. He had an idea to make moving easier. He thought they could use a pulley system to move boxes up an inclined plane and into a truck instead of carrying the boxes to the truck. He knew that most ramps are made of surfaces that are not slippery, so that people can walk on them without falling. He wanted to make a slippery surface for his ramp so that the boxes would slide up easily. He decided to make a small model to test different surfaces.

1. If you were Jasper, how would you make your model? Draw a picture, labeling the parts and indicating the size of each part.

2. What kinds of materials could Jasper test? _____
_____
_____

3. What could Jasper use as a load to pull up his model ramp? _____
_____
_____

4. What could Jasper measure to test the different surfaces? _____
_____
_____
_____

5. How could Jasper decide which surface worked the best? _____
_____
_____

Compare and Contrast

Machines That Make the Same Trade

A screw and an inclined plane look very different and are often used for different types of work. A screw has a spiral shape, but an inclined plane is a flat surface. A screw can hold together pieces of wood or metal, but an inclined plane can help people raise or lower objects to a given height.

Screws and inclined planes also are alike. The shape of a screw is actually made by wrapping an inclined plane around a pole. Both machines do work by trading a longer distance for a greater force. A ramp is an inclined plane that makes it easier for people to go from one point to another. A spiral staircase is a type of screw that has the same use.

Fill in the chart, comparing and contrasting screws and inclined planes.

Screws and Inclined Planes

	Compare	Contrast
Shape		
Purpose		

Use with page F88.

How Do Some Other Simple Machines Help Us Do Work?

Lesson Concept

Inclined planes, screws, and wedges are simple machines that help us do work.

Vocabulary

inclined plane (F84)   **efficiency** (F85)   **screw** (F86)   **wedge** (F88)

Match the pictures to the captions, and complete the captions.

A	B	C

1. Inclined plane _____ helps us do work by _____

_____

_____

2. Screw _____ helps us do work by _____

_____

3. Wedge _____ helps us do work by _____

_____

_____

4. What is the relationship among the three simple machines pictured?

_____

5. How could you improve the efficiency of the ramp?

_____

_____

Recognize Vocabulary

simple machines	lever	fulcrum	work
inclined plane	effort force	wedge	screw
wheel and axle	pulley	efficiency	

Fill in the blanks with the letters of the correct vocabulary terms.
Rearrange the circled letters to answer the question below.

1. lever, wheel and axle, pulley, inclined plane, screw, and wedge

  _ _ _ ⚪ _ _   _ _ _ _ _ _ _ _

2. a wheel with a rope or chain fitted around it   _ _ ⚪ _ _ _

3. a flat surface with one end higher than the other

  _ _ _ _ _ _ ⚪ _ _ _ _ _

4. what is done when a force moves an object across a distance   _ _ _ ⚪

5. two inclined planes placed back to back   ⚪ _ _ _ _ _

6. the force you place on a simple machine

  _ _ _ ⚪ _ _   _ ⚪ _ _ _

7. a large wheel attached to a smaller wheel or rod

  _ ⚪ _ _ _ _ _ _ _   _ _ _

8. the result of wrapping an inclined plane around a pole   ⚪ _ _ _ _ _
  ⚪

9. a bar that turns around a fixed point   _ _ _ _ ⚪

10. a fixed point around which a lever moves   _ _ _ _ _ ⚪ _

11. how well a machine changes effort into useful work

  ⚪ _ _ _ _ _ _ _ _ _

What do simple machines do?

_ _ _ _ _ _   _ _ _   _ _ _ _ _

Name _____

Date _____

Write About Simple Machines

Persuasive Argument—Composition

Suppose that you have a friend who thinks simple machines are no longer useful today. On a separate sheet of paper, write a four-paragraph composition in which you try to convince your friend that simple machines are important in everyday life. Your composition should have an introduction stating your argument, two paragraphs supporting your main point, and a brief conclusion. Use the web diagram below to organize your ideas before you begin writing.

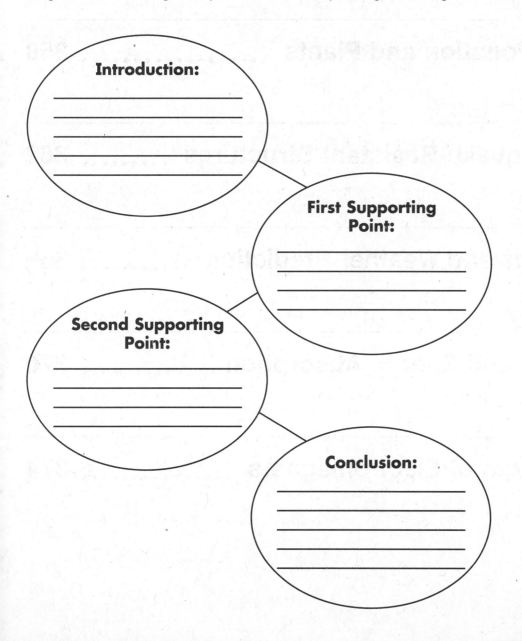

Introduction:
_____
_____
_____

First Supporting Point:
_____
_____
_____

Second Supporting Point:
_____
_____
_____

Conclusion:
_____
_____
_____
_____

Use with pages F94–F95.

Unit Experiments
Grade 4

Experiment Log

Use these pages to plan and conduct a science experiment to answer a question you may have.

1 Observe and Ask Questions

Make a list of questions you have about a topic. Then circle a question you want to investigate.

_____

_____

2 Form a Hypothesis

Write a hypothesis. A hypothesis is a suggested answer to the question you are investigating. You must be able to test the hypothesis.

_____

_____

3 Plan an Experiment

Identify and Control Variables

To plan your experiment, you must first identify the important variables. Complete the statements below.

The variable I will change is _____

_____

_____

The variable I will observe or measure is _____

_____

_____

The variables I will keep the same, or control, are _____

_____

_____

Name _____

Experiment Log

| Develop a Procedure and Gather Materials |

Write the steps you will follow to set up an experiment and collect data.

_____

_____

_____

_____

_____

_____

_____

_____

_____

_____

| Materials List | Look carefully at all the steps of your procedure and list all the materials you will use. Be sure that your teacher approves your plan and your materials list before you begin.

_____

_____

_____

_____

_____

_____

_____

_____

_____

_____

Name _____

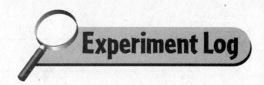

4 Conduct the Experiment

| Gather and Record Data | Follow your plan and collect data. Make a table or chart to record your data. Observe carefully. Record your observations and be sure to note anything unusual or unexpected. Use the space below and additional paper, if necessary.

| Interpret Data |

Make a graph of the data you have collected. Plot the data on a sheet of graph paper or use a software program.

5 Draw Conclusions and Communicate Results

Compare the hypothesis with the data and the graph. Then answer these questions.

Do the results of the experiment make you think that the hypothesis is true?

Explain. _____

_____

How would you revise the hypothesis? Explain.

_____

_____

What else did you observe during the experiment?

_____

_____

Prepare a presentation for your classmates to communicate what you have learned. Display your data table and graph.

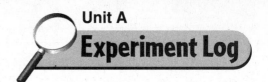
Water Sources and Plant Growth

1 Observe and Ask Questions

Does the type of water used affect how a plant grows? For example, will plants watered with pond water grow taller than plants watered with tap water, rainwater, or bottled water? Make a list of questions you have about plant growth and water sources. Then circle a question you want to investigate.

_____

_____

_____

_____

2 Form a Hypothesis

Write a hypothesis. A hypothesis is a suggested answer to the question you are investigating. You must be able to test the hypothesis.

_____

_____

_____

3 Plan an Experiment

To plan your experiment, you must first identify the important variables. Complete the statements below.

Identify and Control Variables

The variable I will change is _____

The variable I will observe or measure is _____

The variables I will keep the same, or *control*, are _____

_____

_____

Name _____

Experiment Log

Develop a Procedure and Gather Materials

Write the steps you will follow to set up an experiment and collect data.

_____
_____
_____
_____
_____
_____
_____
_____
_____
_____
_____
_____
_____
_____
_____
_____
_____

Use extra sheets of blank paper if you need to write down more steps.

Materials List Look carefully at all the steps of your procedure, and list all the materials you will use. Be sure that your teacher approves your plan and your materials list before you begin.

_____
_____
_____
_____
_____

Name _____

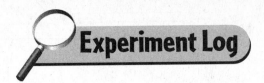
Experiment Log

4 Conduct the Experiment

| Gather and Record Data | Follow your plan and collect data. Use the chart below or a chart you design to record your data. **Observe** carefully. **Record** your observations and be sure to note anything unusual or unexpected.

Plant Observations

Water Source	Height (mm)						
	Day 1	Day 2	Day 3	Day 4	Day 5	Day 6	Day 7

Water Source	Height (mm)						
	Day 8	Day 9	Day 10	Day 11	Day 12	Day 13	Day 14

Observations

_____

_____

Name _____

 **Experiment Log**

| Interpret Data |

Make a graph of the data you have collected. Plot the graph on a sheet of graph paper or use a software program.

5 Draw Conclusions and Communicate Results

Compare the **hypothesis** with the data and graph, and then answer these questions.

1. Based on the results of the experiment, do you think the hypothesis is true?

   Explain. _____

   _____

   _____

2. How would you revise the hypothesis? Explain. _____

   _____

   _____

3. What else did you **observe** during the experiment? _____

   _____

   _____

Prepare a presentation for your classmates to **communicate** what you have learned. Display your data table and graph.

| Investigate Further | Write another hypothesis that you might investigate.

_____

_____

_____

_____

_____

_____

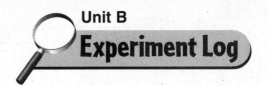
Soil Pollution and Plants

1 Observe and Ask Questions

How does polluted soil affect plants? For example, does a plant growing in polluted soil change in any way? Make a list of questions you have about soil pollution and plants. Then circle a question you want to investigate.

_____

_____

_____

2 Form a Hypothesis

Write a hypothesis. A hypothesis is a suggested answer to the question you are investigating. You must be able to test the hypothesis.

_____

_____

_____

3 Plan an Experiment

To plan your experiment, you must first identify the important variables. Complete the statements below.

Identify and Control Variables

The variable I will change is _____

_____

The variable I will observe or measure is _____

The variables I will keep the same, or *control,* are the _____

_____

_____

_____

_____

Name _____

Develop a Procedure and Gather Materials

Write the steps you will follow to set up an experiment and collect data.

_____

_____

_____

_____

_____

_____

_____

_____

_____

_____

_____

_____

_____

_____

_____

_____

_____

Use extra sheets of blank paper if you need to write down more steps.

Materials List Look carefully at all the steps of your procedure, and list all the materials you will use. Be sure that your teacher approves your plan and your materials list before you begin.

_____

_____

_____

Name _____

4 Conduct the Experiment

Gather and Record Data Follow your plan and collect data. Use the chart below or a chart you design to record your data. **Observe** carefully. **Record** your observations, and be sure to note anything unusual or unexpected.

Observation Log

Plant Label	Plant Height (cm)						
	Day 1	Day 2	Day 3	Day 4	Day 5	Day 6	Day 7

Plant Label	Plant Height (cm)						
	Day 8	Day 9	Day 10	Day 11	Day 12	Day 13	Day 14

Observations

_____

_____

_____

_____

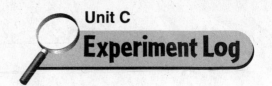
Earthquake-Resistant Structures

1 Observe and Ask Questions

How can you minimize earthquake damage to a building? Make a list of questions you have about the damage caused by earthquakes to buildings. Then circle a question you want to investigate.

_____

_____

_____

_____

_____

_____

2 Form a Hypothesis

Write a hypothesis. A hypothesis is a suggested answer to the question you are investigating. You must be able to test the hypothesis.

_____

_____

3 Plan an Experiment

To plan your experiment, you must first identify the important variables. Complete the statements below.

Identify and Control Variables

The variable I will change is _____

_____

The variable I will observe or measure is _____

_____

Interpret Data

Make a two-column chart. Label the columns "Plant" and "Change." List the plant labels in the first column. Compare your observations from Day 1 and Day 14. Summarize your findings in the second column.

5 Draw Conclusions and Communicate Results

Compare the **hypothesis** with the data and chart, and then answer these questions.

1. Given the results of the experiment, do you think the hypothesis is true? Explain. _____

_____

2. How would you revise the hypothesis? Explain. _____

_____

_____

3. What else did you **observe** during the experiment? _____

_____

_____

Prepare a presentation for your classmates to **communicate** what you have learned. Display your data table and chart.

Investigate Further | Write another hypothesis that you might investigate.

_____

_____

_____

_____

_____

Name _____

Experiment Log

The variables I will keep the same, or *control*, are _____

_____

_____

| Develop a Procedure and Gather Materials |

Write the steps you will follow to set up an experiment and collect data.

_____

_____

_____

_____

_____

_____

_____

_____

_____

_____

_____

_____

_____

_____

_____

_____

Use extra sheets of blank paper if you need to write down more steps.

| Materials List | Look carefully at all the steps of your procedure, and list all the materials you will use. Be sure that your teacher approves your plan and your materials list before you begin.

_____

_____

_____

Name _____

4 Conduct the Experiment

Gather and Record Data Follow your plan and make careful **observations.**
Record your observations, and be sure to note anything unusual or unexpected.
Draw the inside of your model house before and after each earthquake.

House #1

Before the Earthquake   **After the Earthquake**

House #2

Before the Earthquake   **After the Earthquake**

Observations

_____

_____

Name _____

5 Draw Conclusions and Communicate Results

Compare the **hypothesis** with the drawings, and then answer these questions.

1. Based on the results of the experiment, do you think the hypothesis is true?
    Explain. _____

    _____

    _____

2. How would you revise the hypothesis? Explain. _____

    _____

    _____

3. What else did you **observe** during the experiment? _____

    _____

    _____

    _____

Prepare a presentation for your classmates to **communicate** what you have learned.
Display your model houses and your drawings.

Investigate Further Write another hypothesis that you might investigate.

_____

_____

_____

_____

_____

_____

_____

_____

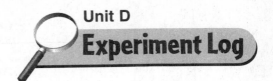
Clouds and Weather Prediction

1 Observe and Ask Questions

Can clouds be used to predict the weather? For example, are feathery white clouds indicative of clear weather or stormy weather? What do layered clouds indicate about upcoming weather? Make a list of questions you have about clouds and their role in weather forecasting. Then circle a question you want to investigate.

_____

_____

_____

_____

2 Form a Hypothesis

Write a hypothesis. A hypothesis is a suggested answer to the question you are investigating. You must be able to test the hypothesis.

_____

_____

3 Plan an Experiment

To plan your experiment, you must first identify the important variables. Complete the statements below.

Identify and Control Variables

The variable I will change is _____

_____

The variables I will observe or measure are _____

The variables I will keep the same, or *control*, are the _____

_____

Name _____

Experiment Log

Develop a Procedure and Gather Materials

Write the steps you will follow to set up an experiment and collect data.

_____
_____
_____
_____
_____
_____
_____
_____
_____
_____
_____
_____
_____
_____
_____
_____
_____

Use extra sheets of blank paper if you need to write down more steps.

Materials List Look carefully at all the steps of your procedure, and list all the materials you will use. Be sure that your teacher approves your plan and your materials list before you begin.

_____
_____
_____
_____

Experiment Log

4 Conduct the Experiment

Gather and Record Data Follow your plan. Make observations of clouds and collect other kinds of weather data. Use the charts below or charts you design to record your data. **Observe** carefully. **Record** your observations and measurements.

Cloud Types and Other Weather Conditions

Observations and Measurements

Week 1	Day 1	Day 2	Day 3	Day 4	Day 5	Day 6	Day 7

Observations and Measurements

Week 2	Day 8	Day 9	Day 10	Day 11	Day 12	Day 13	Day 14

Interpret Data

Make line graphs of the measurements you made. Plot the graphs on graph paper, or use a software program.

5 Draw Conclusions and Communicate Results

Compare the **hypothesis** with your observations and measurements, and then answer these questions.

1. Given the results of the experiment, do you think the hypothesis is true?

   Explain. _____

   _____

   _____

   _____

2. How would you revise the hypothesis? Explain. _____

   _____

   _____

   _____

3. What else did you **observe** during the experiment? _____

   _____

   _____

   _____

Prepare a presentation for your classmates to **communicate** what you have learned. Display your data tables and graphs.

Investigate Further
Write another hypothesis that you might investigate.

_____

_____

_____

_____

_____

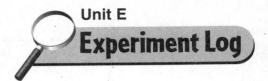
Color and Energy Absorption

1 Observe and Ask Questions

How does color affect the amount of light energy an object will absorb? For example, will a container lined with black paper absorb more light energy than a container lined with white paper? Make a list of questions you have about color and light energy absorption. Then circle a question you want to investigate.

_____

_____

_____

_____

_____

2 Form a Hypothesis

Write a hypothesis. A hypothesis is a suggested answer to the question you are investigating. You must be able to test the hypothesis.

_____

_____

3 Plan an Experiment

To plan your experiment, you must first identify the important variables. Complete the statements below.

Identify and Control Variables

The variable I will change is _____

The variable I will observe or measure is _____

The variables I will keep the same, or *control*, are the _____

_____

_____

_____

Name _____

Develop a Procedure and Gather Materials

Write the steps you will follow to set up an experiment and collect data.

_____

_____

_____

_____

_____

_____

_____

_____

_____

_____

_____

_____

_____

_____

_____

Use extra sheets of blank paper if you need to write down more steps.

| Materials List | Look carefully at all the steps of your procedure, and list all the
materials you will use. Be sure that your teacher approves your plan and your
materials list before you begin.

_____

_____

_____

Name _____

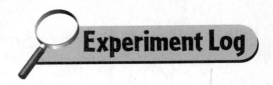

4 Conduct the Experiment

Gather and Record Data | Follow your plan and collect data. Use the chart below or a chart you design to record your data. **Observe** carefully. **Record** your observations, and be sure to note anything unusual or unexpected.

Color and Temperature (Heat Absorption)

Location: _____				Type of Material: _____							
_____				_____							
Heat Source: _____ _____											
Color of Material:	**Temperature (°C/°F) (every 5 minutes for 60 minutes)**										
Control											
	5	10	15	20	25	30	35	40	45	50	55	60

Other Observations

_____

_____

_____

_____

Experiment Log

Interpret Data

Make a graph of the data you have collected. Plot the graph on a sheet of graph paper, or use a software program.

5 Draw Conclusions and Communicate Results

Compare the **hypothesis** with the data and graph, and then answer these questions.

1. Given the results of the experiment, do you think the hypothesis is true?

Why or why not? Explain. _____

_____

_____

_____

2. How would you revise the hypothesis? Explain. _____

_____

_____

3. What else did you **observe** during the experiment? _____

_____

_____

Prepare a presentation for your classmates to **communicate** what you have learned. Display your data table and graph.

Investigate Further Write another hypothesis you might investigate about color or heat absorption.

_____

_____

_____

_____

_____

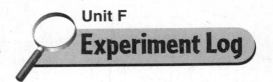
Strength of Electromagnets

1 Observe and Ask Questions

What affects the strength of an electromagnet? For example, if more wire coils are wrapped around an iron nail, will the electromagnet have a stronger electromagnetic pull? Make a list of questions you have about the strength of electromagnets. Then circle a question you want to investigate.

_____

_____

_____

_____

2 Form a Hypothesis

Write a hypothesis. A hypothesis is a suggested answer to the question you are investigating. You must be able to test the hypothesis.

_____

_____

3 Plan an Experiment

To plan your experiment, you must first identify the important variables. Complete the statements below.

Identify and Control Variables

The variable I will change is _____

_____

The variable I will observe or measure is _____

_____

The variables I will keep the same, or *control,* are the _____

_____

Name _____

Experiment Log

Develop a Procedure and Gather Materials

Write the steps you will follow to set up an experiment and collect data.

_____
_____
_____
_____
_____
_____
_____
_____
_____
_____
_____
_____

Use extra sheets of blank paper if you need to write down more steps.

| Materials List | Look carefully at all the steps of your procedure, and list all the materials you will use. Be sure that your teacher approves your plan and your materials list before you begin.

_____
_____
_____
_____
_____
_____

4 Conduct the Experiment

Gather and Record Data Follow your plan and collect data. Use the chart below or a chart you design to record your data. If needed, design additional charts as you test different variables. **Observe** carefully. **Record** your observations, and be sure to note anything unusual or unexpected.

Electromagnet Strength Observations

Wire thickness: _____   Core type (material wrapped): _____

Wire length: _____   _____

Steel object type: _____   Battery size: _____

Number of Loops	Number of Objects Picked Up

Other Observations

_____

_____

_____

_____

_____

_____

_____

Experiment Log

Interpret Data

Make a graph of the data you have collected. Plot the graph on a sheet of graph paper or use a software program.

5 Draw Conclusions and Communicate Results

Compare the **hypothesis** with the data and graph, and then answer these questions.

1. Given the results of the experiment, do you think the hypothesis is true? Explain. _____
   _____
   _____
   _____

2. How would you revise the hypothesis? Explain. _____
   _____
   _____
   _____

3. What else did you **observe** during the experiment? _____
   _____
   _____
   _____

Prepare a presentation for your classmates to **communicate** what you have learned. Display your data table and graph.

Investigate Further   Write another hypothesis that you might investigate.

_____
_____
_____
_____
_____